4/23

Beyond the Burning Bush

Beyond the Burning Bush
Hearing and Answering God's Call

Edited by Vicki Brown, Meg Lassiat,
and Sharon Rubey

With a Foreword by Bishop Minerva G. Carcaño

General Board of Higher Education and Ministry
The United Methodist Church
Nashville, Tennessee

The General Board of Higher Education and Ministry leads and serves The United Methodist Church in the recruitment, preparation, nurture, education, and support of Christian leaders—lay and clergy—for the work of making disciples of Jesus Christ for the transformation of the world. Its vision is that a new generation of Christian leaders will commit boldly to Jesus Christ and be characterized by intellectual excellence, moral integrity, spiritual courage, and holiness of heart and life.

The General Board of Higher Education and Ministry of The United Methodist Church is the church's agency for educational, institutional, and ministerial leadership. It serves as an advocate for the intellectual life of the church. The Board's mission embodies the Wesleyan tradition of commitment to the education of laypersons and ordained persons by providing access to higher education for all persons.

Visit our Web site at www.gbhem.org.

All Scripture quotations unless noted otherwise are taken from the New Revised Standard Version of the Bible, copyright 1989, Division of Christian Education of the National Council of Churches of Christ in the United States of America. Used by permission. All rights reserved.

ISBN 978-0-938162-81-0

Produced by the Office of Interpretation

Manufactured in the United States of America

Contents

If We Listen, We Can Hear God's Voice

In her essay for this book, Amy Barlak Aspey writes, "As I look back, God was whispering to me for many years, but it took a sledgehammer to get my attention. . . . I could not hide from God's call any longer. I realized that while many of my excuses were truthful, none of them were faithful."

This kind of quote inspires me. My primary job is to educate and encourage youth and young adults who are considering a future in ministry. I travel across the country to lead and attend events at which young people gather to share their stories, and I communicate with deacons, elders, boards of ordained ministry, district superintendents, and bishops as they share similar stories. Through Web sites, publications, and personal conversations, I try to bring these great stories to light so that others can benefit from them.

God calls, and individuals respond in many creative and exciting ways. As more and more resources, time, and conversations are dedicated to encouraging young people to consider ordained ministry as their vocation, I am excited about what the future holds. According to The Lewis Center for Church Leadership, in the fall of 2008 the percentage of United Methodist elders under the age of thirty-five rose above 5 percent (to 5.2 percent) for the first time this century. Additionally, the percentage of young adult deacons rose to 7.7 percent.

This is good news, but there is still room for improvement, and there are many exciting possibilities ahead. Whenever God's call is heard and the listener responds, an extraordinary sequence of events is set in motion, inside and outside of traditional church settings. Regardless of age, gender, ethnicity, or setting, God calls all of us. Some are called to ordained ministry. All are invited to respond.

As you read these stories, you will see time and time again the importance of individuals introducing or affirming for someone that God is calling them to ministry. Through the voices of parents, friends, church pastors, or other mentors, God speaks to those God calls and invites them to consider a new direction in their lives.

Perhaps you know someone you could invite to consider that God is calling them to serve through their vocation. One thing we know is that almost all of those who serve in ordained ministry today do so because a trusted mentor or friend encouraged them along the way. Leadership is passed from one generation to the next through the trust and encouragement of experienced leaders who identify and support those who will lead the future generations.

How can you help encourage someone who may need to hear that God is calling them? We hope that this book will be one tool you can use to encourage others as they discern God's call. And if you believe God is calling you, we hope you will find inspiration and hope in the stories collected here.

This collection is a clear example of how—if we listen—we can hear God's voice in many different ways and respond creatively through both traditional and nontraditional ministries. I commend these writings to you and thank those who shared in such compelling ways the story of their journey to hear and respond to God's call. I believe many readers will find in these stories a new sense of calling, or at the very least, a renewed, resounding affirmation of God's call in their lives.

Yours in ministry,

—The Rev. Meg Lassiat

Director of Student Ministries, Vocation, and Enlistment

Division of Ordained Ministry

General Board of Higher Education and Ministry

The United Methodist Church

Nashville, Tennessee

Foreword

The Church Will Always Be My Home

Minerva G. Carcaño

I was helping my father replace the flooring in my own Sunday school classroom when I believe God began to speak to me about my call to ordained ministry. I had begged my father to allow me to go to church with him to help him with the task. I told him that I could be a big help to him, but the truth was that I simply loved going to church. It did not matter what activity was occurring at my home church, or whether nothing was occurring. Already, at age five, I simply felt drawn to church.

I can still remember the old vinyl flooring, cracked and dried from age. I helped my father as he rolled it up and pushed it over to one end of the room. There it was, an old roll of broken, cracked, dirty vinyl lying on the floor beside an upright, bright, and shining brand-new roll of flooring. After the hard work of removing the old flooring, my father asked me to sit on the floor between the old and the new flooring while he went to his car to fetch a tool he needed. I found a clean, smooth spot, and sat down.

I could still hear my father's footsteps as he walked down the hallway of that small wooden educational building when God visited

---

I could still hear my father's footsteps as he walked down the hallway of that small wooden educational building when God visited me. No, I didn't see God or hear God. I felt God. It was as if the whole room suddenly filled with God's presence. I felt embraced by God's own love and my heart began to beat with incredible joy!

---

me. No, I didn't see God or hear God. I felt God. It was as if the whole room suddenly filled with God's presence. I felt embraced by God's own love and my heart began to beat with incredible joy!

I was too young to articulate what I had experienced, but even in my tender heart I knew what I had felt. That afternoon I felt divine love and Holy Spirit joy, but there was something else. I felt that I was home. It was a homecoming and I knew then and there that the church was and always would be my home. From that day on, I began to think about how I could live in God's house, my home.

In third grade, I thought I had figured it out.

In Sunday school, I saw a picture of a female missionary in our class materials and I thought, "I'll be a missionary!" I thought being a missionary would allow me to live in God's house. Even though it was only a picture, it was the first time I had seen a woman living her life in full-time service to God, and I was inspired to do the same! Because I spoke Spanish, I thought I might become a missionary to Latin America. I had heard of the great needs of Latin America, and I was ready to go to serve God and to serve others.

A few years later, when I joined the youth group of my church as a twelve year old, I met another woman who was serving God, a deaconess in a church community center. She made me aware of the fact that I did not have to leave my area of the world in order to serve others. I was already part of a community that had great social and economic needs.

I admired this woman very much. Her faith reminded me of the faith of my grandmother, who had taught me to read with her Spanish-language Bible.

At the end of the day, my grandmother would find a passage of Scripture and ask me to read it. I would usually be sitting at her feet or by her side as she knitted, crocheted, or mended socks and torn work shirts for my uncles. After I had read the passage she and I would sit in silence. Then gently she would ask, "What do you think the Bible is telling us? What do you think Jesus wants us to do? What did you learn?"

When we had finished our conversation about the Scripture passage we would pray together, asking God to help us live according to God's Word. Both my grandmother and the deaconess of my early youth taught me the importance of striving to live according to God's Word. However, it was a pastor who lived God's Word with the fullness of his life who eventually led me to ordained ministry.

Growing up Hispanic and poor in a time when even the church was clearly segregated and prejudiced formed me in ways that left me insecure and unsure of my own self-worth. In this pastor, I came to know one of God's own prophets. He would preach God's justice on Sunday morning and then on Monday challenge the racism of our local school system, as well as the racism of our denomination.

He mentored young people and taught us to love God and love neighbor, and hope for God's own reign of justice, mercy, and peace.

God used him to open my eyes to what the world could be because of Christ Jesus. I began to do all I could to serve God and everyone around me. I was on fire as a disciple of Jesus Christ. One day this pastor turned to me and said, "You would make a fine pastor's wife." But God was already at work in my heart and was leading me to ordained ministry instead.

When at age fourteen I told my parents God was calling me to ordained ministry, my father became angry and told me that women were not called to ordained ministry. My mother, who had always encouraged my discipleship, just sat there and cried. Later, she would tell me that she knew how difficult ordained ministry was for men and could only begin to imagine how difficult it would be for me as a woman. Because I am a woman, I did find it difficult to convince men and women that God was calling me to ordained ministry. I did not need to worry so much, for God did convince my father, my pastor, the board of ordained ministry, and the clergy of my conference! I give God thanks that in ordained ministry I am truly home.

As United Methodists, we believe that God calls each and every one of us to ministry in the name of Jesus Christ. In this call to ministry, some of us are set apart for ordained ministry. Ordained elders are called by God to lead God's people in Word, Sacrament, Order, and Service, thus serving in the church and in the world. Ordained deacons are called by God to Word and Service so they will be able to embody, articulate, and lead the whole people of God in its servant ministry. There is no doubt, however, that all of us are called to the ministry of all believers. It is that sacred task of sharing the good news that others too may become disciples of Christ Jesus and the world may be transformed by his mercy and grace.

Those of us who have had the great privilege of sharing our stories of call in this book pray that our stories will encourage you to share your own story of where God has called you to serve. If you are still discerning God's claim upon your life, may our stories in all of their diversity help you to consider the special call God has for you.

Minerva G. Carcaño was elected to the episcopacy in 2004 and currently serves as the episcopal leader of the Desert Southwest Annual Conference. As the first Latina bishop in The United Methodist Church, she has a long history of committed involvement in ministries with immigrants and refugees, the poor, and U.S./Mexico border communities.

I Ran, But I Couldn't Hide From God's Call

John Michio Miyahara

I grew up in Denver, Colorado, in the early 1970s, when there was no cable or satellite TV. There were the three major networks, PBS, and a few local stations for a total of five or six television stations.

In those days a really popular television show was *Mission Impossible*. The movie with Tom Cruise is based on that show, which starred Peter Graves. One night my parents let me stay up past my bedtime to watch the first ten minutes. The KGB, the Soviet secret police, had bugged the room Peter Graves's character was in with listening devices. He was knocking on the wall to uncover the hidden "bug."

A few days later, I became convinced the KGB was spying on me, too. I had no idea why the KGB would want to spy on a seven-year-old in Denver, but I began to knock on my bedroom wall looking for a bug. I took a hammer and gave the wall a solid whack. I was surprised to learn that the KGB was *not* spying on me.

I knew my mom would not be happy with the hole in my wall. I needed to hide the hole. On my dresser I found my Cokesbury Sunday school flyer from the previous week. Inside the flyer there was a pullout poster of a Scripture verse: "But I say to you, Love your enemies and pray for those who persecute you, so that you may be children of your Father in heaven" (Matthew 5:44-45).

I used that verse to cover the hole, and God used the verse to remind me of an important Scripture lesson that I saw every day until my room was repainted a few years later. Like the prophet Jeremiah, God's prevenient grace is working in our lives even at a young age. God was already taking steps in my life to make an impression on me and to grab my attention.

Today, I have a daily ritual. I put on my class ring from the Boston University School of Theology, where I finished seminary. It reminds me of several things. First, this is a new day to celebrate life. Second, I am called once again to ministry. Third, in accepting the call, I realize that regardless of what the day holds, I make a covenant to do this for God. Lastly, I am reminded that my calling is not just about me—it is about how I live out my Christian, Wesleyan faith in the world as a disciple of Jesus Christ.

As I have read many call stories from clergy of many ages over the years, I have noticed the following:

- Each call story is individual and unique
- There is no set formula or rubric to be called by God to ordained ministry
- God calls many people—men and women, young and old, of all different backgrounds, at different times in their lives
- God calls whom God calls—sometimes the most unlikely person
- Discerning a call to ministry is a process
- One cannot be an ordained minister without a clear sense of calling.

My own call took many years for me to discern. I ran away from it many times. However, the many communities of faith I lived in supported and helped me grow into and accept my calling.

During the 1994 EXPLORATION event, the late Bishop Cornelius Henderson said, "Sometimes a call to ministry is like an itching that you just can't scratch." I can't convey to you how true these words have been to me and how they guided me in my early journey of discerning my call.

I first heard my call to ministry at age sixteen, driving with my parents from California back home to Colorado after attending United Methodist Asian-American summer camp. On the drive home, as we pulled into Salt Lake City to spend the night, I had a deep, internal, overwhelming sense that God wanted my attention. At first, this feeling was confusing and overwhelming.

Several weeks later, I wrote a letter to Pastor Tom Choi, who was the director of Asian Camp. I told him about my experience of sensing God wanting me to do something. When Tom wrote me back he said, "Maybe God is calling you to ministry."

Romans 10:14-17

But how are they to call on one in whom they have not believed? And how are they to believe in one of whom they have never heard? And how are they to hear without someone to proclaim him? And how are they to proclaim him unless they are sent? As it is written, "How beautiful are the feet of those who bring good news!" But not all have obeyed the good news; for Isaiah says, "Lord, who has believed our message?" So faith comes from what is heard, and what is heard comes through the word of Christ.

That line shocked and scared me.

At sixteen, there was no way that I ever thought of being ordained. Ordained ministers are really religious, serious, very smart, and pious people, I thought. Not traits that seemed to relate to me.

My image of a minister was the Rev. Paul Hagiya, who was the pastor of my family's church for seventeen years. At Simpson United Methodist Church, my home church, the Rev. Paul was almost a saint. He had a great presence that was both authoritative and compassionate.

Ministers are *geeks!*

As I pondered what the camp director said about God calling me, as well as my image of pastor in my own family's pastor, I thought there is *no way* I could be a pastor. Not only did I lack the qualities of a pastor, at the age of sixteen, I was involved in Distributive Education Clubs of America and wanted to go to college, and then Stanford University School of Business to get an MBA, make millions of dollars by the time I was thirty, and live in a great condo on the beach.

To convince myself of why I didn't want to be an ordained minister, I made this list:

- Ministers are *geeks!*
- All ministers wear polyester suits and collars. Who wants to wear that?
- I want an MBA from Stanford School of Business and a BMW 5 Series.
- Seminary! *Ugh!* All that reading and writing pastors do on top of Bible study and preaching. Yuck!

The call lingered through high school and college. I graduated from Loyola Marymount University in Los Angeles, still uncertain what to do with my life. I halfheartedly applied to the Iliff School of Theology in Denver. I could live with my parents and figure out what I wanted to do with my life. I figured I could do seminary for a year, quit, and say I tried.

The plan almost worked.

I quit seminary after one year and worked for the next year at three jobs. First, I did a rural ministry internship in Sultan, Washington. Second, I worked for the HIV/AIDS unit of the Colorado State Department of Public Health. And finally, I worked at the Johnstone Center—a home for people with physical and mental disabilities.

I really believe that God gave me that year to figure out that, although I did good work at these jobs, it was not work I was passionate about or "called" to do for the rest of my life. The inkling, the "itching that I just couldn't scratch," came back and would not go away. I knew God was not going to leave me alone!

On May 9, 1991, my life changed as I submitted. As I was driving home from work, I had come to the certain realization that I was called to ministry, though I was scared to finally acknowledge this fact to myself. I briefly looked up as I was driving and said aloud, "OK God, I will do this ministry thing, but I cannot do it alone, and I still have to be me."

Submitting my life to God and answering my call to ordained ministry was one of the hardest things I have ever done. At the same time, it was the most liberating. I knew where to focus the direction of my life. I also knew the road would continue to be challenging, but that I was not going alone, as God through Christ journeyed with me.

Since my ordination, I have been fortunate to serve in many places and settings. I have been with families as the quiet, still, and powerful presence of God that is in hospital rooms at the time of a death, after a person has heard bad, life-changing news, at Columbine High School, at Arlington National Cemetery, after the terrorist attacks of 9/11, and in the aftermath of Hurricane Katrina. I have been there to help people rebuild their lives and find hope. I am the joyful, enthusiastic presence of God that celebrates at the birth of a child, baptisms, confirmations, weddings, graduations, anniversaries, and other milestones. I have been a teacher, preacher, theologian, ethicist, reluctant prophet, pastor, priest, evangelist, missionary, counselor, and chaplain to countless communities in country churches, in urban churches, on college campuses, and in military communities.

Being an ordained minister has not always been easy, but I have never regretted answering my call to ministry.

Is God calling you? If so, will you join me?

Step-by-step, God is leading some of you into the vocation of ordained ministry.

For some of you, the call is clear and the step forward is as well. For others it is not so clear; or like me, you may be hesitant to move forward.

Do you feel a call, an inkling, or even an "itching that you just can't scratch" that may be God calling you to ordained ministry? I challenge you to pray, to listen, and to take steps forward in order to hear and discern more clearly "the call."

If God calls you to ordained ministry, step out on faith and scratch that itch. You won't be alone!

John Michio Miyahara is a native of Denver, Colorado, and an elder in the Rocky Mountain Annual Conference. He began his theological education at the Iliff School of Theology and completed it at the Boston University School of Theology. Currently the director of Religious Life and Community Services at Dickinson College in Carlisle, Pennsylvania, he is on a three-year leave of absence and in a three-year recall in the U.S. Navy, serving as the senior Navy chaplain at Arlington National Cemetery.

EXPLORATION

Here's a chance to spend three days with other young people— high-school seniors through those age twenty-four—who are exploring ordained ministry. EXPLORATION is an informative and discerning weekend of worship, Bible study, prayer, workshops, and small-group discussions. The event is held on a regular basis, as a national event in some years and by jurisdiction in other years. If you have sensed that God might be calling you to ordained ministry, wondered what ministry in The United Methodist Church is all about, would like some help sorting through the issues surrounding a Christian vocation, or want to find out more about United Methodist seminaries and theological schools, this gathering is for you.

All baptized Christians are called to ministry. EXPLORATION may help you discover if your call might be to the ordained ministries of Word, Sacrament, Order, and Service in the church. For information, visit www.gbhem.org/exploration.

John Miyahara preaches at Exploration 2006, telling the story of his own call, which took years to discern.

God Does Not Call Us to Do Great Things Alone

Diane Winters Johnson

T oday I am an ordained deacon. I say the words again, "I am an ordained deacon." They sound good in my ear and feel right in my heart. The fit is well in my soul. I think about the path that has brought me here—not one that I have walked alone. Six years ago, as I stood on the stage at annual conference with my guide dog beside me and answered the questions as the bishop asked them, I also thought about the path that had brought me there.

I traveled in ministry with a gregarious yellow dog, Walter. (Amber is the name of the dog I have today.) We were a ministry team. My responsibility was to tell him where we were going and stay on top of where we were by providing good directions and navigation details. His responsibility was to guide me around obstacles and keep us traveling in a relatively straight path. Most of the time this worked out quite well and we got where we needed to go in good order.

Together, we accomplished what I could not do alone. Ministry is like that. God does not call us to do great things alone.

My earliest memory of church includes standing beside my grandmother on a summer Sunday morning, listening to people singing hymns, smelling the musty wood aroma of the ancient building, and feeling the warmth of the summer sun shining through the windows. I felt completely surrounded by love—a unique and special love that was my relationship with God.

My next intense personal contact with God came when I was thirteen years old and enrolled in a confirmation program. My parents seldom attended church, but believed I needed a solid foundation of faith. One particular session, I arrived early and was sitting alone in the sanctuary singing quietly and waiting for the others to arrive when I became aware of a presence and knew I was not alone. My tears fell as the warmth of the sun poured through the windows and the overwhelming sense of peace and divine love made my soul feel complete. I knew at that moment that God had work for me to accomplish on this earth and had written God's name on my heart. Since that time I have heard God calling in the night, in the morning, through Scripture, through worship, through others, and through my family. My call has been clear, it has been strong, and it has been undeniable.

But as I grew up and followed a traditional path of marriage and family, that path included a slow loss through my young adulthood that resulted in blindness. How would I answer God's call if I couldn't cross the street by myself? How could I preach God's Word if I couldn't read the Bible by myself? These questions created self-doubt, and for more than a decade I struggled with discerning God's calling. My family and my church provided strength and affirmation of the presence of the Holy Spirit in my life as I continued to acquire the skills I needed to live and work independently.

I attended church weekly throughout my adult life. I have always felt the presence of God in the sanctuary and heard the angels singing with the choir. Through worship, God has been there tugging at my heart a number of times. My ministry in the church has included both volunteer and paid staff positions and it was through my ministry experiences that I realized God was indeed calling me

How would I answer God's call if I couldn't cross the street by myself? How could I preach God's Word if I couldn't read the Bible by myself?

to ordained ministry. People in the church have come to me for help, support, and acceptance. Through this experience, I have felt God's gentle direction in my life. Others have seen God using me and have supported and affirmed each decision I have made regarding my work within the church and my path toward ministry.

As I began talking with my pastor and the district superintendent about declaring my candidacy for ordained ministry, two important realizations came to the forefront. At this point in time I was a "cane traveler," meaning I used a long white cane to detect obstacles on the ground as I walked. The difficulty this method presented for me in ministry was that it limited my independence in travel. A long cane connects the traveler to the ground and the focus remains low and around the perimeter of a room or around the edges of a space. The horizon for me was limited. There had to be a better way.

A friend convinced me to consider a guide dog. Soon I left for The Seeing Eye in Morristown, New Jersey, and graduated with my new guide, Walter. As I learned to walk with Walter the whole world opened up in new ways. Travel with a guide dog changes the horizon from the limited low floor or edge, as with a cane, to the wide outward expanse through the eyes of the dog. Now I was ready to begin the challenges of ministry.

I began to explore important questions about exactly what kind of ministry God intended for my life. Was I to be an elder or a deacon? The answer to the question came to me in a simple way. I spent more than a year seeking the advice and counsel of friends, colleagues, teachers, family, my pastor, my district superintendent, and just about anyone who could offer me insight. The truth, however, rested deep within me. I needed to discover my authentic voice in order to discover my authentic identity in ministry.

I considered the ministry that elders were ordained to do: preach the Word, administer the sacraments, order the church, and serve the poor and needy. I was certainly capable of doing all of these things. God had given me many gifts to help me in these areas of ministry. Then I considered the ministry that deacons were ordained for: preaching and teaching the Word of God and serving God's people in the church and in the world. That's it. For one, the elder, God had given the church for safekeeping. But God remembered that there are other children. There are those who exist in the margins of the church and in society who somehow escape our reaches, and so in response to the poor and the marginalized, the church created the order of deacon. God sent the deacon to the ones in the margins.

Both the elder and the deacon love the church and love God's people, but they serve God and the church in unique ways. Where would I find my authenticity in interpreting God's call in my life? As I considered my gifts for ministry with the reality of both my abilities and my limitations I knew that I was able to follow either path. I could be an elder and lead a church, but whenever I found myself serving in that role I felt stressed and tended to worry. The end of the day could never come soon enough.

Likewise, I knew that I had the ability to be a deacon and serve the church and God's people outside the church as well. When I served in this capacity, I was completely unaware of time. I lost myself in the ministry and was completely present with the people and situations in which I found myself. This was how I knew that God's call for me was to be an ordained deacon.

I am currently on staff at Wooster United Methodist Church as a deacon with responsibility for mission and Christian education. I also serve as a community services liaison in our work with the poor of our community. I love our people and live for the Lord. My work is rewarding and challenging. It is my breath.

God's call came to me in an instant that day so long ago when I was a young girl. It launched me on a path of self-examination and discovery that led me to this place. However, God has not been silent in the intervening years. God has been calling me over time, continuing to whisper my name. I believe God will continue to call me all the days of my life. I can't wait to discover where we will go.

Diane Winters Johnson is an ordained deacon in the East Ohio Conference of The United Methodist Church at Wooster United Methodist Church. She lives and works in Wooster, Ohio, with her husband, Wes, and her Seeing Eye dog, Amber. Diane graduated from Ohio State University and The Methodist Theological School in Delaware, Ohio, with a master's degree in Christian education.

Bishops William Morris, left, and Dick Wills ordain Laura Kirkpatrick as a deacon.

Who Are Deacons?

Deacons are persons called by God, authorized by the church, and ordained by a bishop to a lifetime ministry of Word and Service to both the community and the congregation in a ministry that connects the two.

What Does a Ministry of Word and Service Mean?

Deacons devote themselves to the ministry of the Word, which includes sharing, teaching, and modeling the Word of God.

Additionally, deacons are called to a lifetime of servant leadership, serving both the congregation and the world. This service is manifested in many ways, including:

- forming and nurturing disciples;

- leading the congregation's mission to the world;
- leading the congregation in interpreting the needs, concerns, and hopes of the world;
- leading in worship and assisting the elders in the administration of the sacraments of baptism and Holy Communion.

Additionally, for the sake of extending the mission and ministry of the church, a bishop may grant local sacramental authority to the deacon to administer the sacraments in the absence of an elder, within a deacon's primary appointment, and in conducting marriages and funerals.

A deacon is called to serve all people, particularly the poor, the sick, and the marginalized, and to equip and lead the laity in ministries of compassion, justice, and service. The deacon's leadership role exemplifies Christian discipleship, equips and supports all baptized Christians in their ministry, and connects the church's worship with its service in the world.

Where Do Deacons Serve?

Deacons can serve a variety of appointments. In local churches, deacons model, teach, and lead in equipping others to live out servant ministry and to serve others in and out of the church. In appointments beyond the local church, deacons serve or lead in a ministry of compassion and justice.

How Do Deacons Find Work?

Deacons' appointments are approved by the bishop. However, unlike elders, their appointments may be self-initiated, initiated by an agency seeking their service, or initiated by the district superintendent or the bishop. They are not guaranteed an appointment. Instead, they search for their own positions, giving them the freedom to make changes when needed. Once they find a position, they ask the bishop to approve their appointment.

God Is in the Midst of Our Questions and Insecurities

Jonathan Fell

n the anxiety of moving to Chicago, beginning seminary, and understanding my place in my new community, I met with a small group of students for class in a small, musty, yellow room across from the Chapel of the Unnamed Faithful at Garrett-Evangelical Theological Seminary. Still bewildered, and physically beat from the beginning of the semester, we were asked to share our call stories with one another. From around the circle of small desks reminiscent of those that populated the classrooms of my high school came stories filled with tragedy, visions, divine revelation, and audible calls from above.

Listening as my classmates shared, I began to fear the story of my call, a story of slow growth, would be as exciting as a garden show to a drag racer. I felt as though my call was missing something in comparison. Lifting my hand from the desk to wipe my forehead,

I noticed a perfect imprint of my palm set in condensation on the desk in front of me. I was scared that my inability to articulate my call and the fact that my story lacked the grandiosity and thrill of the stories of my classmates meant I was somehow unfit for ministry.

And if that was the case, why had I moved to Chicago in the first place? As my turn to share finally came, I could do nothing but simply tell my story in all its anticlimactic wonder.

The process of articulating my call has been challenging. My call has been a gradual but deliberate process over the past several years and I have come to understand most as my "call" only in retrospect. Throughout my adolescent years, I had several experiences and made several decisions that led me toward answering that call. The biggest or most memorable of these experiences involve great movements of the Spirit and deliberate decisions on my part, but all have significantly affected my life and my faith in God.

I grew up in the United Church of Christ. My family and I attended a small church in Iowa City, Iowa, called Faith. Faith United Church of Christ was where I learned about God and what it meant to live a life of faith. As a child, I attended Sunday school with great regularity, spent portions of my summer at church camp, and learned the importance of being in community and mission with others. My church family encouraged and empowered me to make my faith in Christ my own. That had a profound impact on my life of faith and on my call to ordained ministry. My church family showed me what it meant to extend the love of God to others. They taught me about the overwhelming love of Christ. They taught me what it meant for Jesus to eat with tax collectors and associate with prostitutes. They loved me when I found it hard to love myself, and it was that love that I wanted to share with others.

One morning on my way to church I broke down in tears. The insecurities and stress of my adolescent life had become too much for me to bear, and as a result I could no longer conceal the emotional baggage I had fought so hard to contain. As I got out of the car and made my way up to the door of the small, brown church, my tears became unstoppable. In a futile attempt to hide the wet blotches of red covering my face, I pushed my way through the foyer full of congregants sipping coffee and raced down the hallway. Making my way past coatracks and stacks of folding chairs, I made a beeline for the farthest and most secluded place I could think of: the boiler room.

Inside, the air was thick with the smell of dust, musty mops, and cleaning supplies scented by artificial citrus. The giant heater in the middle of the room made the air humid and uncomfortable, but I took comfort in the fact that its hum would drown the sound of

I have come to understand most of my "call" only in retrospect.

my sobs to those in the hall. I shut the door behind me and left the lights off, hoping to remain as inconspicuous as possible. Alone, lit only by a faint glow of sunlight making its way through the dust on the glass of a forgotten window in the back of the room, I attempted to compose myself.

Then, without warning, the door opened behind me. Entering silently, my pastor put her hands on my shoulders and gently shushed my crying. Turning around, my eyes, still blurred with tears, met hers. After what seemed like hours, she broke the monotonous babble of the heater. I cannot remember what she said; the words of her prayer are as lost to me as was the reason why I was crying in the first place. Regardless, the power of that moment, the great sense of calm I felt overcome me, has left an imprint deep within my muscle memory. My tears were gone so quickly I could do nothing but laugh.

I took a great deal from that experience. And though I have a real memory of what the love of God can do, there is so much more to a life of faith than a single experience. I have never had an experience quite like that since; but I have cried since then. I have met myself in places of doubt and fear in which an experience like the one I had in the boiler room of that small church would have been overwhelmingly welcome.

Yet, faith is not and cannot be a crutch to which we cling. Faith must be that which we use to inform, guide, and aid ourselves as we deal with the complexities of life. I have learned to take comfort in the fact that doubt and questioning have been built into my faith in God. I take comfort because regardless of what happened in my life, for better or worse, God was and will be helping me through. Sure, life in retrospect is easier to understand and I recognize that questioning faith can be uncomfortable and maybe even a bit dangerous. But God is in the midst of our questions and insecurities of faith; we just have to have the courage to be vulnerable and to acknowledge and experience God's presence.

Since that experience, I have made several decisions that have been significant in the discernment of my call to ministry. I transferred my membership to The United Methodist Church, I chose to study religion at a secular state school, and I supplemented my work in religious studies with a degree in English. And though many students "fall away" from their faith during college, I could not deny the fact that I was called by God to be in ministry. I discovered that my love for literature was not a way around exploring my call into ministry. I found a way to challenge my faith, not only through my classes in the religious studies department but through literature and story as well.

With respect for our shared Christian tradition, and the thousands of years of Christian history, my faith is my faith. No one will ever share what I have experienced in my relationship with God in the exact same way. Calls are as varied as those who receive them. Some calls are seemingly verbose while others are nothing more than a movement of the Spirit. Some are sudden and automatic while others, like mine, are gradual and require discernment. And regardless of the delivery, all calls are as ever changing and ever growing as those who receive them.

As Paul reminds us, "There are varieties of gifts, but the same Spirit; and there are varieties of services, but the same Lord; and there are varieties of activities, but it is the same God who activates all of them in everyone" (1 Corinthians 12:4-6).

I have come to understand the gentle nudging of pastors and fellow congregants for me to lead Bible studies and worship as part of my call to share the Word of God. I have come to understand a quiet prayer, in a humid storage room, spoken with pastoral compassion as part of my call to extend God's love to others. I have come to understand my love of literature and story as a means through which I might be able to continually learn how God interacts with us, and how we interact with God.

Though the story of my call may not be as flashy as those of some of my colleagues, through all of these experiences I have grown to understand my call to serve God by sharing the gifts, knowledge, and love that God has shared with me with those around me. My call has been long and not without discernment, but I have come to understand the necessity for the time I have spent not knowing. Though I do not always appreciate the uncertainties, it is the uncertainties that continue to drive my desire for further education and new experiences. I am called to be in ministry. The question now is what will that ministry look like?

Jonathan Fell is a member of St. Mark's United Methodist Church in his hometown of Iowa City, Iowa. He received his B.A. in religious studies and English at the University of Iowa in 2007 and is currently in his second year at Garrett-Evangelical Theological Seminary in Evanston, Illinois. He was cochair of the 2007/2008 United Methodist Student Movement Steering Committee.

The United Methodist Student Movement

Christian students' strong legacy of leadership in The United Methodist Church spans generations. The current United Methodist Student Movement (UMSM) is carrying on that tradition. Students have a voice and an important role in the church. The movement seeks to be an all-inclusive and diverse community connecting university and college students through the unifying love of Jesus Christ.

Student Forum is the annual UMSM gathering, held each

To find out about the UMSM and Student Forum, go to www.umsm.org.

May on different college campuses. Some 500 students and campus ministers come together, representing annual conferences across the United States. Key pieces of the event include leadership training, theological reflection, faith enrichment, spiritual formation, worship, voluntary service, and education about social issues. It's a forum for ecumenical involvement with other students as well as a place to discuss and articulate students' vision for The United Methodist Church.

The Many Voices of God's Call Were Loud and Clear

Julienne Judd

Y ou were baptized on the third Sunday in May, and you were eight months old. I was standing right beside your mother and father, and the pastor who baptized you," my godmother said. My godmother would then extend her hands as if she was holding an infant, continuing, "And you were just so." My godmother took her covenant with God seriously, reciting this story to me over and over as I was growing up. She never failed to pray with me every time she saw me, and upon our parting, she would always say, "Now don't forget you're a Methodist."

I believe that God has been calling me since the moment I was born, when my mother prayed for me in the delivery room. In my years as a pastor, I have not met too many people who can recite the day they were baptized as an infant, who baptized them, and who was in attendance. The fact that I can leads me to believe the

The Rev. Julienne Judd officiates at a wedding.

importance of that moment in time for me. I also believe it was another voice of God calling me.

God's voice was loud and clear as my mother would tell me about the amazing moment when she witnessed the Damascus road experience of her grandfather as he chose to walk "the Jesus road." She would tell me stories about old-time preachers who were bilingual, who would simultaneously translate the message that the late Bishop Angie Smith preached into the many Native languages of their people, or stories of the Methodist Caravans that came and led summer meetings and Bible school. She spoke of her great-uncle, the late Rev. Matthew Botone, who would make four and five trips back and forth to church with kids packed into his car each trip, so they could have vacation Bible school. His wife, Hazel Botone, would later become a local pastor. All these stories are a part of who I am and the calling on my life.

My father's great-uncle, the Rev. Joshua Wesley, who was a Baptist preacher, his wife, Leona, my grandmother, my dad, and the many Choctaw singers continued to be the voice of God calling me as I watched and listened to them play Southern gospel music on the piano, as well as sing in their own language. Even now all I have to do is hear a song and I can see them all again. As I hear their voices, I also hear God.

Many people do not realize that many tribes or nations have a long history of Christianity. I often am asked, "What is your tribe's traditional religion?" I then reply, "How far do you want to go back?" I come from a long line of people of faith, five generations of clergy and lay leaders, on both sides of my family. I went to church at the Baptist church and the Methodist church interchangeably, as hard as that is to imagine! I think that's why my godmother was so adamant about my remembering I was Methodist.

I loved church, Bible school, Sunday school, singings, revivals, camp meetings. Everything about church was like breathing or eating. It still boggles my mind to think how one can live without the fellowship of Christ's disciples.

When I was ten years old I attended a Southern Baptist camp meeting. I don't even remember the sermon, or what song was being played, but as we were standing for the invitation, I only remember the evangelist asking, "Is God calling you for special service to him? Is he speaking to your heart right now?" At that moment, I knew what I was called to be. I remember shakily making my way down the long aisle to the front, to the long line of preachers and realizing I knew only one, my mother's former campus minister and friend. I remember walking to him. As he took my hand, he asked, "Is God calling you for special service?" I immediately answered, "Yes, he's calling me to be a preacher."

Ignorance is bliss, I have been told. I realize now he could have said, "Maybe God's calling you to be a home missionary or a Sunday school teacher, or to the mission field," or he could have just told me that little girls in the Southern Baptist Church could not grow up to be preachers. Instead, he knelt down with me, raised his head to the sky, and laughed a holy laugh that filled me with such joy that I started crying and didn't know why.

His prayer for me was "Lord, give her her heart's desire." I can still hear his voice and the sound of his laughter, which was the voice of God's joy as I responded to the call. It was not until three years later that I experienced for myself the understanding of my baptism, and God's forgiving grace.

I met my husband and married when I was very young. His father was an Assemblies of God pastor, and eventually my husband became a pastor. I loved being a pastor's spouse, but I always wanted my husband to try different ways of teaching and I wanted him to develop new programs. I loved helping him, though I am sure he didn't always consider me helpful. It was another twelve years before I finally gave up trying to avoid what Jeremiah 20:9 so aptly describes: "If I say, 'I will not mention him or speak any more in his name,' then within me there is something like a burning fire shut up in my bones. I am weary with holding it in, and I cannot."

In the meantime, we raised our four children, and my husband transferred to The United Methodist Church and became a local pastor. I went back to school, taught Sunday school, worked at youth camp, and at the urging of the United Methodist Women became a lay speaker. I taught at schools of mission. I now understand that each opportunity was God using a different voice to call my name.

One Sunday on Women in the Pulpit Day, I made a presentation to the congregation. Afterward, one of my husband's parishioners said, "You just might be the next pastor." I quickly replied, "After being a pastor's spouse, there is not enough money in the world to make me be a pastor."

Famous last words. The reality is there is not enough money to "make" anyone become a pastor. What I know now is that we serve God out of our love for him in response to his overwhelming love for us.

I declared my candidacy in 1987, but declaring candidacy and actually becoming a candidate are two separate things. Being a Native American woman in a white conference had its own difficulties, as I pushed the edges of comfort. My files were lost on two consecutive visits with the board of ordained ministry. Prior to my third appointment I used all my money to make twelve copies of my files. To this day I am not quite sure what followed, but I eventually became a candidate under Bishop Dan Solomon. My husband and I then transferred into the Oklahoma Indian Missionary Conference and became their first clergy couple.

As a second-career minister, with my children all in high school, I chose the Course of Study path at St. Paul School of Theology. The day my name was read at the annual conference session—I found peace in my soul.

I have pastored rural Native American churches with predominately one tribe, urban churches, Native American churches with as many as twenty-seven tribes and nations; was a campus minister to a Native American Wesley Foundation; and campus minister to a Native American university. When I hear clergy from other conferences talk about cross-cultural appointments, I think of myself and my clergy brothers and sisters in the Oklahoma Indian Missionary Conference and laugh quietly to myself.

I am beginning my nineteenth year as a pastor and have been an elder for twelve years. Although I might regret bad choices I have made in life, I have not regretted one moment of my choice to follow the calling. With all the struggles—personal, political, financial, health, racism—I still wouldn't trade it for anything in this life, only in the next one.

As the call continues today, I still hear God's voice through my parents, siblings, husband, children, grandchildren, friends, and church family. My godmother has been gone three years now. Her life and the way she lived it was only one of many of God's voices that called to me.

My godmother was the first lay delegate to be seated from the Oklahoma Indian Missionary Conference at General Conference in 1972. Yes, I will remember I am a United Methodist.

Julienne Judd of the Kiowa Tribe of Oklahoma and Choctaw Nation of Oklahoma is an ordained elder in the Oklahoma Indian Missionary Conference and pastor of three Native American congregations in Kansas.

The Voice of the Lord Called Me to Dillard

George Kimbrough Johnson

My sophomore year of college I attended a state university in Louisiana, where I experienced racism that made me believe that I wasn't wanted there. I was told by the university staff that I had been under surveillance for hanging out with my African-American friends who were on the football team. When David Duke, former Grand Dragon of the Ku Klux Klan, was invited to come and speak at the university, I knew that I had to leave. I just didn't know what to do.

My grandfather suggested his alma mater, Dillard University, a historically black United Methodist-related university in New Orleans. I dreamed I saw pretty white buildings and a duck pond and I knew I was supposed to go to Dillard University because it has both of those. Even as I became excited about my new university, another part of my life was filled with sorrow.

My mother had contracted spinal meningitis. When I visited her in the hospital, she told me to go to New Orleans and have a fun time. I said that I would. On March 24, 1991, Palm Sunday, at the age of forty-six, my mother went to be with the Lord.

While I was in the limousine on the way to the cemetery I heard the voice of the Lord ask me, "Who are you going to go to now?" I responded by saying that I had no one to turn to but God. I was nineteen, and returned to my state school to finish the semester. While there, I applied for admission to Dillard University. Around this time I had another experience that influenced my call to ministry.

I met two female custodians on campus who were members of the Church of God in Christ. As we spoke, they began to tell me that I had the mark of God upon my head. When I heard this, I was afraid, and I went to my dormitory room and tried to rub it off. They then invited me to go to church with them. When I attended the services the members prayed for me, which prepared me for my transition to Dillard University in the summer of 1991.

In June 1991, I arrived on the campus of Dillard University. I soon met many new people, including a young lady who invited me to go to the French Quarter and hang out. When we got there, we went to several bars and had many drinks. After a long evening we went to catch the bus back to campus only to find out that the buses had stopped running for the night. My newfound friend told me she would go and call some of her friends to pick us up. While I was waiting for her, I sat on some steps that faced a cathedral. A man came and sat near me on those steps, and we began to talk. He said to me, "You know what, boy, one day you are going to be a preacher!" I immediately became sober and contemplated his statement as I left.

Shortly thereafter, I heard the voice of the Lord tell me to change my major from education to religion and philosophy. I was further instructed that if my grandparents opposed this, I was to tell them that I was going to drop out of school. When I explained to them that I was changing my major, they objected until I told them that I was going to drop out of school. I did well as a religion and philosophy major, making my grandfather proud when, like him, I graduated cum laude.

Just before graduation, I was in the cafeteria discussing with my friends the possibility of attending seminary. One of my friends said to me that I didn't have to worry about that because her father was the president of a seminary. I laughed, and she said that she was serious. I told her "OK," and asked her to set up a meeting. Sometime later I was taking a nap in my room and heard a knock at the door. I was told that there was a man who wanted to see me. Once I went out I met the late Reverend Dr. Kenneth B. Smith, who was the president of the Chicago Theological Seminary. He invited me to apply. I was accepted and received the Presidential Prize Fellowship, which helped me accept God's call to ordained ministry.

George Kimbrough Johnson is an emerging faculty fellow at Dillard University. He is the former pastor of Bethel United Methodist Church of Queen City, Texas, and St. Paul United Methodist Church of Jefferson, Texas. He is the former chaplain and instructor of religion at Wiley College in Marshall, Texas.

The Black College Fund

The Black College Fund provides support for the eleven historically black colleges and universities related to The United Methodist Church. These schools were among those founded after the Civil War with the primary objective of educating those newly freed from slavery. Because of the importance of these institutions in giving hope to those often denied access to higher education, the 1972 General Conference established the Black College Fund as an apportioned general church fund. To learn more about the Fund, visit www.gbhem.org/bcf.

THE BLACK COLLEGE FUND
The United Methodist Church

For Me, Faith and Justice Are Inseparable

Rebekah Jordan Gienapp

I cannot point to one single experience that led to my accepting the call to become an ordained deacon so God could use me to seek justice with people who are poor. There were so many people and places that helped me discover this call that I cannot name them all. As a college student, I came to know and volunteer with many people from a variety of Christian traditions—people who taught me that faith and justice were inseparable. Serving with them caused me to read the Bible with new eyes, seeing themes of poverty, wealth, and justice woven throughout the Scriptures I had been hearing all my life without fully absorbing.

Through my college's campus ministry, I began to organize students to take action against hunger by lobbying with an ecumenical organization called Bread for the World. As an intern with Bread, I found a deep sense of satisfaction in teaching Christians about Scripture's teachings on poverty and hunger, and giving them concrete opportunities to put these teachings into action. I began to discern that I had a vocation to seek justice with people who are poor and with other people of faith. I began to consider enrolling in seminary after college, though I did not think about ordination. I felt strongly that I needed to learn more about theology, biblical studies, and ethics in order to help other Christians connect faith with justice. But when I thought of ordained ministers, the examples I knew of were parish pastors and chaplains, and neither of these seemed to fulfill the calling I felt.

There's a name for what I'm called to do.

Fortunately, my father, an elder who is a chaplain, brought me materials to read for those who were considering ordination. It was 1997, just one year after General Conference created the Order of Deacons as another means toward ordination. When I read profiles of deacons, and learned that deacons were called to connect worship with ministries of love, justice, and service in the world, I thought, "There's a name for what I'm called to do." I began to consider how ordination as a deacon would allow me to bring the ministry of The United Methodist Church to places in my community where Christian voices for justice were greatly needed.

I enrolled as a student at Garrett-Evangelical Theological Seminary with a clear sense of call to the deacon's order, but I was still unsure what particular setting would allow me to seek economic justice. The field education director at Garrett pointed me to Interfaith Worker Justice, a national organization based in Chicago. I was assigned to work on a project organizing faith community support for workers in poultry plants in the South who were trying to organize unions because of the debilitating injuries, low wages, sexual harassment, and disrespectful treatment that they often experienced in the workplace. Traveling to rural communities in Arkansas, North Carolina, Georgia, and Delaware opened my eyes to how abusive some low-wage workplaces can be. I began to consider how many jobs in our nation keep workers mired in poverty, rather than lift them out of it.

Having grown up in Memphis, Tennessee, I was certainly no stranger to the problem of widespread poverty. I also knew from my experiences as a white person that racism was still very much alive in my city, and that the most frequent form it took today was economic. Nearly forty years after Dr. Martin Luther King Jr. died in our city defending the rights of sanitation workers to earn a living wage and to join a union, low-wage African American workers, as well as a growing number of Latino workers, were still suffering in the workplace. I saw churches that were struggling to provide adequate charitable services to people who were employed.

These same churches needed a vehicle for speaking and working for justice, so that fewer hardworking people would be forced to rely on charity while they worked at low-wage jobs. I was reminded that Jesus' first sermon in Luke is one in which he proclaims that the Spirit of the Lord has anointed him "to bring good news to the poor. . . . [T]o proclaim release to the captives and recovery of sight to the blind, to let the oppressed go free, to proclaim the year of the Lord's favor" (Luke 4:18-19). I believed that if this was at the forefront of Jesus' ministry, it should also be central to our churches' ministries today.

My last semester of seminary, I prepared for commissioning and my return to the Memphis Annual Conference. With the support of Interfaith Worker Justice and a number of United Methodist and ecumenical partners, I made plans to begin a local affiliate of Interfaith Worker Justice called Workers Interfaith Network in Memphis.

Rebekah Jordan Gienapp and others at a rally for a living wage.

The Parable of the Widow: Luke 18:1-8

Then Jesus told them a parable about their need to pray always and not to lose heart. He said, "In a certain city there was a judge who neither feared God nor had respect for people. In that city there was a widow who kept coming to him and saying, 'Grant me justice against my opponent.' For a while he refused; but later he said to himself, 'Though I have no fear of God and no respect for anyone, yet because this widow keeps bothering me, I will grant her justice, so that she may not wear me out by continually coming.'" And the Lord said, "Listen to what the unjust judge says. And will not God grant justice to his chosen ones who cry to him day and night? Will he delay long in helping them? I tell you, he will quickly grant justice to them. And yet, when the Son of Man comes, will he find faith on earth?"

The day after I returned from annual conference, I went to my new office at the Workers Interfaith Network. I started to figure out what was needed to organize the faith community around specific campaigns that would result in workers earning living wages and working in safe and respectful conditions.

As the organization began to build relationships across denominational and faith lines, and with union and community partners, we decided to focus on two areas: passing a living wage ordinance, and supporting low-wage workers at a warehouse who were trying to establish a union. These campaigns got to the heart of the problems that keep low-wage workers in poverty: being paid wages that cannot sustain a family, and not having a voice in the workplace— decisions that so deeply affect their lives. Both of these campaigns were also complex, difficult, and lengthy. As a growing number of people supported these campaigns, we learned the lesson of Luke's persistent widow: only by seeking justice until we've risked "wearing out" corporate and political decision makers will social change happen (Luke 18:1-8). After three years of supporting the warehouse workers, they won a contract with their employer that improved their wages and working conditions. After almost four years of lobbying, our city council adopted our living wage ordinance.

Though God's call to seek economic justice has been clear in my life for many years now, the path that the clergy, laity, and workers I work with would be asked to take has not always been clear. There have been surprises, both good and bad, and many lessons learned as some of our organizing has succeeded, while some of it has failed. What God has confirmed time and again is that the church is asked to walk outside its doors so that it can follow Christ in seeking justice in the world.

Rebekah Jordan Gienapp is a deacon in the Memphis Annual Conference and executive director of the Workers Interfaith Network (founded as the Mid-South Interfaith Network for Economic Justice).

Visualizing God's Way for My Life

Paul Perez

I have long found the concept of "call" and "calling" a difficult one. I know that it has deep roots in the Scriptures and tradition of the Christian church. Jesus, so long ago, called to fishermen, "Come follow me." Today, the same Christ calls to each of us, beckoning us to follow him. But, whenever I hear the term, all I see, in my mind's eye, is a phone ringing and someone picking up, answering: "Hello? . . . Oh, hello, God. . . . Yes . . . yes. Ah, so you want me to be a preacher. . . . Got it. . . . Thanks for the call." For me, the language of call is far too neat and tidy. It evokes the idea of receiving clear instructions and following them to the letter. As I have sought to be faithful, to follow Christ, I have found that my following has led me to new, surprising, and unplanned places. Recently, in reflecting on my "calling" I have realized that I prefer the idea of "vision" over "call."

The language of vision, for me, speaks to the need for imagination, creativity, and dreaming for the vocation of ministry. Images communicate things that speech cannot, touching not only our minds but our hearts. Vision captures, for me, the mysterious and holy ground on which we encounter the Triune God. A vision comes to us in the present moment with a profound glimpse of God's future and challenges to see and imagine our lives in radically new and exciting ways. It is with this mind that I want to share some of my visionary experiences that have led me to follow more intently and authentically the beacon of Christ in my life.

On a dark night, during that strange, in-between summer that connects high school and college, I was running in my neighborhood when I suddenly stopped in my tracks and stared with frightening intensity at the sky. I had been thinking about my future as I pounded down the sidewalk—thinking about the uncertainty of the coming months as I moved away from home, thinking about the expectations of my loved ones and how I simultaneously longed to live up to them and rebel against them, thinking about a new love kindled with a girl moving a state away. As these thoughts flooded my mind, I simply stopped, looked up and, peering beyond the fuzz of my suburban neighborhood, my suburban life, caught a glimpse of the star-filled sky, of the deep and immense universe in which our small and fragile planet is nestled. And yet, in addition to this, I caught a glimpse of something else.

There, in my mind's eye, I saw flash before me a vision of what my life could be, should be, would be, if I surrendered it to God and followed Christ. I can't explain this vision; it is something that defies words. Catching my breath from the miles run, I whispered, "I get it—I see what can happen if I follow you."

To be clear, this experience did not happen in a vacuum. A few years before I had undergone a powerful conversion experience while participating in an Appalachia Service Project work team sponsored by my local church. Prior to leaving for the trip I was convinced that the poor, rural, and ignorant people of Appalachia would, in prejudice and discrimination, single me out because of my Mexican heritage. In preparation, I practiced how I would self-righteously respond to their ethnic slurs. My host family, however, accepted my team and me with radical hospitality and love, and welcomed us into their home and their life. At the end of the week, a member of the family embraced me and through tears whispered, "I love you."

Recently, in reflecting on my "calling" I have realized that I prefer the idea of "vision" over "call."

This family embodied Christ's love in my life, exposing my deeply rooted prejudice, my sin. That summer I came to understand, in a real and personal way, my need for God's saving and transforming grace. Returning home, I shared my experience during a Sunday service, after which my pastor suggested I think about ordained ministry. A seed was planted, but I was reticent in nurturing it. I had long been encouraged by my parents to pursue a career as a medical doctor, and by my senior year of high school I was toying with counseling or social work. Becoming an ordained minister just did not fit with my vision of the future.

My experience that summer night overturned my vision of the future, challenging me to imagine my life in a new way: God's way. Fast-forward to the summer before my final year at Michigan State University—and I again faced a visionary experience. I had become deeply involved at Michigan State's Wesley Foundation, serving as a peer minister, and serving on the national steering committee of the United Methodist Student Movement. My involvement in both these communities challenged me to open my eyes to God's vision for my life. That summer, I served as a mission intern for the Detroit Annual Conference. In our training, the facilitator handed us small cards with different icons of Christ and challenged us to take time and pray with our icon. I received the "Good Shepherd"—a picture of Jesus with a lamb over his shoulders. As I sat and stared prayerfully at the icon, I found that I began to understand myself as that lamb slung across Jesus' shoulders, and I began to surrender myself to the shepherding of Christ in my life.

This visionary moment of surrender, submission, and obedience was crucial in my decision to attend seminary after college. Since I, rather falsely, believed that seminary was just for people preparing to be pastors, I decided to start at Wesley Theological Seminary with the plan of pursuing ordination as an elder. But even this plan was turned upside down. After marrying that girl who had so inconveniently moved a state away five years earlier, I found myself troubled by my choice to be ordained an elder. I began to deeply consider the Order of Deacons. I believe that this restlessness was the nudging of the

Paul Perez talks with church member Ron Fadoir during Newberg United Methodist Church's "Do Good Sunday." Church members divided up into teams and worked on service projects in the community.

Holy Spirit to see in the deacon's ministry a perfect place for my gifts and passions. The deacon's ministry connects the church and the world by asking, in words and deeds, if there is, indeed, such a division.

As I discussed my malaise with my wife, Anne, one summer night on our apartment balcony, she turned to me and said, "Paul, it sounds like you just need to make a decision." Her words went straight to the heart! I realized that I had made a decision, that I had made a plan, but it was not my decision or my plan that I need to follow; it was God's. My two visionary experiences returned to me and challenged me to ask am I following God?

Today I am a commissioned deacon and working on a doctorate in church history—a far cry from the vision of the future I had for myself some ten years ago. Who knows what the next ten will bring? After all, this is why responding to the call or vision of God is so exciting. Following Christ wherever he leads is an adventure full of the unexpected and even the dangerous. It challenges us to be courageous in the face of failure and humble in the face of triumph. It leads us into ever-deepening relationship with God and our neighbor.

Paul Perez is a commissioned deacon and serves at Newburg United Methodist Church in Livonia, Michigan, and is a graduate student at the Catholic University of America.

God Got My Attention With a Sledgehammer

Amy Barlak Aspey

Occupation is a popular topic of conversation in high school. All my friends wanted to be teachers, engineers, or health-care professionals. Through middle school and junior high, I believed that I was destined to be a doctor, specifically a geriatric specialist. That changed when I was sixteen.

Apparently, God had different plans.

I was always active in my youth group, but had never considered becoming an ordained minister. Even when people at church made remarks such as, "I could see you as a pastor," or "You have definite gifts for ministry," I never took them seriously. I always said, "Thank you very much, but I want to be a doctor." I don't know if I ever *really* believed that I would be a doctor; something about it never felt completely right. It wasn't until ministry felt "right" that being a doctor felt wrong.

As I look back, God was whispering to me for many years, but it took a sledgehammer to get my attention. During my sophomore year of high school, I went on a mission trip with my youth group to Appalachia. It was one of the most amazing experiences of my life. We were working with a group called Appalachia Service Project (ASP), which repairs homes that are in such poor condition that the houses are nearly unlivable.

I was working with a predominately male team and our project was replacing the foundation of a house. One afternoon when most of the guys were off mixing cement, I persistently asked my senior pastor if I could get started breaking the foundation. His response consisted of only a huge smile because he didn't think I was strong enough to handle the task. This was a logical assumption because the sledgehammer weighed fifty pounds, which was exactly half my

Like the prophet Jeremiah, I was convinced that I was too young to go into ministry. I thought that God must have gotten some signals crossed.

body weight. I, however, was not good at being told that I couldn't do something.

After much persistence, he gave in. My pastor handed me the sledgehammer and said, "Fine, Amy, go ahead." I paused for a moment, focused my energy, and then something surged inside of me. I swung the hammer so hard that an enormous chunk of foundation cracked away. I fell to the ground and everyone else just stared. I knew that I didn't swing that hammer by myself. Everyone else realized this too.

Amy Barlak Aspey and members of Trinity United Methodist Church visited Samara United Methodist Church during a mission trip to Russia.

God had my attention, but like many people before me, I responded by making excuses. Like the prophet Jeremiah, I was convinced that I was too young to go into ministry. I thought that God must have gotten some signals crossed. There must have been some mistake. Over and over, I asked myself why me? Since I couldn't answer that question, I continued to explore becoming a doctor.

A doctor at my church knew that I was interested in the medical field and offered to let me shadow him for a day. I eagerly accepted this offer and thought this experience would finally confirm what I was supposed to do with my life.

It did, but not in the way I expected. The doctor allowed me to follow him as he made rounds. He introduced me to the patients by explaining the purpose of my following him around. Most of the patients thought it was cute that I was "playing doctor" for the day.

Jeremiah's Call

Now the word of the LORD came to me saying, "Before I formed you in the womb I knew you, and before you were born I consecrated you; I appointed you a prophet to the nations." Then I said, "Ah, LORD GOD! Truly I do not know how to speak, for I am only a boy." But the LORD said to me, "Do not say, 'I am only a boy'; for you shall go to all to whom I send you, and you shall speak whatever I command you. Do not be afraid of them, for I am with you to deliver you, says the LORD." Then the LORD put out his hand and touched my mouth; and the LORD said to me, "Now I have put my words in your mouth. See, today I appoint you over nations and over kingdoms, to pluck up and to pull down, to destroy and to overthrow, to build and to plant." The word of the LORD came to me, saying, "Jeremiah, what do you see?" And I said, "I see a branch of an almond tree." Then the LORD said to me, "You have seen well, for I am watching over my word to perform it." The word of the LORD came to me a second time, saying, "What do you see?" And I said, "I see a boiling pot, tilted away from the north." Then the LORD said to me: Out of the north disaster shall break out on all the inhabitants of the land. For now I am calling all the tribes of the kingdoms of the north, says the LORD; and they shall come and all of them shall set their thrones at the entrance of the gates of Jerusalem, against all its surrounding walls and against all the cities of Judah. And I will utter my judgments against them, for all their wickedness in forsaking me; they have made offerings to other gods, and worshiped the works of their own hands. But you, gird up your loins; stand up and tell them everything that I command you. Do not break down before them, or I will break you before them. And I for my part have made you today a fortified city, an iron pillar, and a bronze wall, against the whole land—against the kings of Judah, its princes, its priests, and the people of the land. They will fight against you; but they shall not prevail against you, for I am with you, says the LORD, to deliver you.

(Jeremiah 1:4-19)

One patient, however, said something striking. She was an attractive woman in her early sixties who had just lost her husband and was experiencing a variety of aches and pains. As I sat listening to her, I couldn't help thinking that she reminded me of my grandma after my grandpa died. She, too, experienced aches and pains after his death. Her body wasn't hurt; her heart was broken.

The doctor was understanding and said that he might be able to prescribe something that would help. As he left to fill the prescription, something inside me felt compelled to talk to this woman who was a complete stranger. Before I knew what I was saying, I said, "Ma'am, I hope you don't mind my saying so, but you remind me a lot of Grandma after my grandpa died. She hurt, too, but after awhile things got better." She looked straight into my eyes and said, "Thank you, dear. You are going to make a wonderful doctor."

I knew at that moment that I didn't want to help heal bodies; I wanted to help heal souls. Maybe being an ordained minister wasn't such a crazy idea after all.

For the next few weeks, I mulled the idea over in my mind. Then the most incredible thing happened. After I returned home from school one afternoon, my mom mentioned that she needed to talk with me. Immediately, I was concerned because she had gone in earlier that morning for an MRI. Ever since a serious car accident several years before, it was routine for her to go to the doctor for various checkups and I was scared she was going to inform me that something was wrong. My mother is extremely claustrophobic and, therefore, detests getting MRIs. She said, however, that today was different.

During the procedure, when she usually has trouble breathing, she felt very calm and heard a voice, which she believed was God's. The voice said, "I am pleased with Amy's decision." She asked me, "What does that mean?" I froze. I knew what that meant. I was going to be an ordained minister.

Two days later, I began the United Methodist candidacy process.

I could not hide from God's call any longer. I realized that while many of my excuses were truthful, none of them were faithful. Why did I think that God didn't know whom God was talking to? God knew. God created me; God formed me in my mother's womb. God knows me more deeply and more intimately than I know myself. If God wanted someone else to do the job, God would have asked someone else.

As much as I wanted this to be all about me, I began to understand that when God calls, it is *not about us*; it is about what *God will do through us*. We do not have to be able, but we must be available. We have to be willing to step out in faith.

When we step out, however, we must remember that God never leaves us alone. We are not called without being equipped for the journey. God's promise to Jeremiah has offered me assurance many times. In response to God's call, Jeremiah attempted to use an old cop-out. God's response, however, is full of hope.

God said to Jeremiah: "Do not say, 'I am only a boy'; for you shall go to all to whom I send you, and you shall speak whatever I command you. Do not be afraid of them, for I am with you to deliver you." God makes the same promise to Jeremiah that God made to Moses and that God makes to us today. God makes the *promise of presence*: God with us. God tells us to not be afraid of the task before us, because of the God who is *with* us. We have no reason to fear because God will *not* leave us alone.

God is with us each step of the journey.

Following God's call has been, and continues to be, an adventure. I'm never certain what the next step will be. When I entered seminary, the specifics of my calling were unclear. I never felt called to youth work or being a missionary abroad, or at peace with the idea of serving as a senior pastor.

During my Methodist polity class, however, the Holy Spirit spoke to my heart when we were discussing the Order of Deacons. I was struck like a lightning rod. Why had I never considered this path before? Why had I never even *heard* about this before? This was it! Since I have responded to this calling of servant ministry, my heart has been at peace. I have also felt truly alive. I believe God calls each of us to a ministry and that we feel most human, most in touch with the Spirit within us, when we respond to what our Creator is calling us to do.

In June of 2007, I was ordained a deacon in The United Methodist Church. As I reflected on my call, I realized that early on I had asked the wrong question. Instead of asking "Why me?" I should have asked "Why *not* me?" I can't imagine doing anything else.

Amy Barlak Aspey, an ordained deacon, serves as the minister of small groups and missions at Trinity United Methodist Church in Columbus, Ohio. She is a graduate of Princeton Theological Seminary, where she earned her M.Div., and Ohio Northern University, where she graduated with a dual major in religion and professional and organizational communications.

I Heard God Speak Through Scripture

Shonda Jones

Having been unchurched most of my life, one day I dusted off an old, black, tattered Bible I found in our cluttered garage in South Oak Cliff, a neighborhood in Dallas, Texas. It was late at night and a time in which I had suffered tremendously due to multiple abusive situations as an adolescent. Out of my woundedness, that night I prayed to God, "If you are real, I need you. Can you save me from *this*?" As I opened the Bible, I flipped through many pages and my eyes became fixated on the lamentations found in the Psalms as well as the Gospel according to John.

I recall being led to Psalm 139:1-3, which declares, "O LORD, you have searched me and known me. You know when I sit down and when I rise up; you discern my thoughts from far away. You search out my path and my lying down, and you are acquainted with all my ways." It was as I read this Scripture that I accepted Jesus as Lord and Savior of my life, and it is also this psalm that remains a hallmark in my ministry. I discovered words that not only expressed my deepest despair but at the same time these words gave me a new language of hope. It was God's prevenient grace that first prompted me to want to understand who God is and to seek God's will. It was through Scripture that I heard God speak. My discernment process was an inward journey of not only searching the Scriptures but of prayer and meditation.

Within the next year or two, I prepared to enter college at Texas Christian University (TCU) in Fort Worth, Texas. I became involved in a local Church of God in Christ and later a Baptist church in the city of Fort Worth. I surrounded myself with other Christians and slowly learned the language of my new faith. It was in college that I became the founder and president of Word of Truth Gospel Choir led at the time by the now popular contemporary gospel artist Kirk Franklin. My work with the choir caused me to explore, for the first time, my leadership potential.

This potential was later honed by my campus minister, the Rev. Luther Felder. He provided me with sound counsel and introduced me to The United Methodist Church. By God's grace, I became the first person in my family to attend and graduate from college. This would be the springboard from which I could hear God more clearly and where I could be surrounded by those who could aid in clarifying God's call on my life. The voice of God continued to speak to my soul and I received validation from friends, mentors, and my local congregation.

Two years after graduation, I enrolled in the master of divinity program at Brite Divinity School at TCU. During my theological education, I officially became a member of The United Methodist Church by joining St. Luke "Community" United Methodist Church. This decision came after familiarizing myself with *The Book of Discipline*, and long discussions with Rev. Zan Wesley Holmes Jr.

and Dr. Rebekah Miles about the doctrine, polity, and history of The United Methodist Church. I was at home not only with the basic Christian affirmations of the church but also with the distinctive Wesleyan emphases. God actively guided my path using many people as agents of liberation, justice, and love.

I have been called by God to servant leadership as an elder—a calling to Word, Sacrament, Order, and Service. At age twenty-three, I was set on a journey to respond to my call to ordained ministry. While in the candidacy process leading up to probationary membership and commissioning, the Board of Ordained Ministry arranged for my involvement in covenant groups and mentoring to support the practice and work of my ministry as a servant leader, "to contemplate the grounding of ordained ministry, and to understand covenant ministry in the life of the conference."* This support was decidedly one of the most crucial parts of my path toward ordination. It provided me space to discuss ministry with peers and an ordained minister. As a result of self-reflection, conversations and prayers with colleagues in ministry, and prompting by the Holy Spirit, my vocation as an ordained minister begin to take shape.

My current appointment to Emory University's Candler School of Theology as assistant dean of Admissions and Financial Aid is an incredible place for ministry. It is a setting where I and others meet God, converse about God, and commune with God, in the classrooms and hallways of the academy as we tend to the important task of educating and preparing creative and faithful leaders for the church and world. My experience in ministry has affirmed my understanding of God, but in some ways has expanded and enlarged my notions of who God is. The more I am in relationship with God, the more of a glimpse I garner of how the Divine operates in my life and in the lives of those I serve.

My ministry at Candler frequently includes talking to prospective students about theological education, accompanying individuals in their discernment process, evaluating applicants for suitability to

Shonda Jones teaches a Contextual Education Reflection Seminar at Candler School of Theology.

our programs, providing counsel and encouragement to enrolled students, and being an active part of the worshiping community through teaching, preaching, and assuming a sacramental role in the life of the school.

In the years of my ministry, I noticed other gifts that include the gift of presence, encouragement, hospitality, leadership, and discernment. As I give attention to these gifts, I realize that it is not on my own accord that these gifts are demonstrative. Rather, God is deserving of all the glory because of God's grace and mercy. I understand that any gifts are meant to be shared for the fulfillment of God's reign in this world today. Therefore, my gifts are not only to be thought of as an individual enterprise but also as gifts that impact communities.

While I am excited and feel called to serve in this type of extension ministry, I believe that any ministry for which I am engaged comes out of the local church. I provide leadership in a congregational setting as well as in my extension ministry setting.

This has afforded me an opportunity to be connected in congregational ministry and for much-needed spiritual growth and nurture.

In these recent years of ministry, I think about extension ministries in new ways. Oftentimes, I think of Wesley's commitment to serve God's people wherever he encountered them. Now I reflect on his words, "I look upon the world as my parish," with new fervor. Indeed, God has called me to serve in what might be deemed by some as an unlikely place. But for many who need to encounter God's messenger, not just in the walls of the local church but also in the academy, I will present. For after all, it was through the generosity of spirit of someone serving beyond the local church that I came to know God better and was able to respond to my call to ministry.

Therefore, I will continue to say yes to God as I respond to this call to ordained ministry and be open to wherever that leads me. What a joy to be a part of the ministry formation for those who will soon provide leadership for the church. I count it a privilege, and yet another example of God's gracious activity in humanity that God chooses me and that I continuously choose God.

Shonda Jones is an ordained elder in The United Methodist Church from the North Texas Annual Conference. She is an assistant dean of Admissions and Financial Aid at Emory University's Candler School of Theology, and is involved in recruitment, admissions, financial aid, and student life. She is the national adviser to the General Board of Higher Education and Ministry's Young Adult Seminarians Network (YASN).

* From *The Book of Discipline of The United Methodist Church*, 2008.
  Copyright © 2008 by the United Methodist Publishing House; ¶326, page 228.

Serving God and God's People Is My Burning Desire

David James Moreno

When I first started to deal with my call to ordained ministry I asked several clergy members in my conference how they knew they were called. Naively, I thought all would have the same story, but I was surprised that everyone had a different story. I expected to hear that they all had a one-time, powerful, spiritual experience in which God told them they were called to become ordained ministers. This misguided assumption hindered my ability to respond to my calling because I felt that I had not heard God's voice telling me I was called. What I understood was that I had a burning desire to serve God and God's people, to serve in a way that would be defined by a full-time commitment, a vocation that only ordination would provide.

I never heard the voice that I expected I would need to hear calling me to ordained ministry.

A major complication to my hearing that voice was my self-perception. I could not believe that God could be calling a person like me. I have several learning disabilities: dyslexia, dysgraphia, dyscalculia, and attention deficit disorder are some that have been diagnosed. It really doesn't matter what they are called because when I was a child, learning disabilities were not recognized. Yet these learning difficulties affected me greatly. Through all of elementary school, I essentially could not read; my writing was illegible; and I could not do math problems with more than two digits in them.

The teachers in the Roman Catholic school I attended simply "diagnosed" me as dumb. The teachers had no reservations about letting my classmates know their opinion as well. Many times I was publicly humiliated because I could not solve the math problem on the chalkboard correctly, answer a question about our reading assignment, or spell the words the teacher assigned. If I asked questions in class, teachers deemed them too dumb and irrelevant to answer, and once again I would be humiliated in front of my classmates with a disparaging remark.

On one occasion, to save myself from further humiliation, I went to the teacher's desk to ask a question. I do not remember the question I asked; however, it angered the teacher, and I was hit across the face with a hardcover book. I went back to my desk and cried out loud. The teacher came to my desk, picked up a coat from the girl sitting in front of me, and put it over my head. The whole class saw this, and I ended up being humiliated again, in an extremely painful way.

I could not understand why these Christian teachers treated me this way. Even at that young age I understood their abusive manner was ungodly. I understood that these teachers were not acting in the image of God. Their actions did not reflect the image of a loving God that I had seen in my family, particularly in my mother, who was a wonderful reflection of God's love and grace.

Still, I believed my teachers and my peers. I knew I was dumb. It was completely instilled in me. I was dumb; my self-esteem was shattered. I had to repeat second grade, which made my situation even more difficult. Insults and physical abuse from my peers increased. Similar embarrassing incidents continued to occur through-

As I reflect on my young adult experiences I realized I had been trying to respond to God's call in my life through service opportunities. Embracing this knowledge, I was at peace with my place in God's creation.

out elementary school. It was not until the sixth grade that my academic skills began to improve.

In the early 1960s, when I went through elementary and secondary school, students were often passed to the next grade level without basic skills needed to perform academic requirements. With the exception of my second-grade year, I was passed from grade to grade every year. I graduated from high school by taking classes like home economics, wood shop, drama, and speech instead of regular classes such as junior- and senior-level math and science.

San Antonio Community College was the only college that would accept me. The community college had a program for students like me, students who lacked basic academic skills for college. I was enrolled in classes that were noncredited but taught basic skills such as math and English. One of the main components, and the best benefit of the college program, was that it taught me study skills.

That was enough to get me through many classes. However, my disabilities were too great, and for the next fifteen years I was on and off of academic probation, and in and out of college.

After all those frustrating years of failure, my wife, Ginny, convinced me to be tested for learning disabilities. When the results came in, for the first time since elementary school I realized that I was not dumb. I had learning disabilities, and I could learn coping skills necessary to help me obtain my bachelor's degree.

As a young adult, I would not consider ordained ministry as an option for my life vocation. But I was drawn to opportunities to love and serve God and God's people. I volunteered at a drug rehabilitation center, children's recreation organizations, and handicapped learning and recreation programs. This is when I was introduced to The United Methodist Church and youth ministry. This was the setting that provided me the opportunity to discern God's call in my life.

When I asked one of the pastors how God revealed his call to ordained ministry, he answered it this way: "I had a burning desire to serve." He continued, "The desire was so strong it could only be answered by being an ordained minister." I could relate to that and for the first time I understood that God was calling me to ordained ministry because I, too, had that burning desire. As I reflect on my young adult experiences I realized I had been trying to respond to God's call in my life through service opportunities. Embracing this knowledge, I was at peace with my place in God's creation. I fully understood I was called to serve God and God's people through being an ordained minister.

Through the many years I was working on my degree, I found it hard to believe that I wasn't dumb, even though I was clinically diagnosed with learning disabilities. The belief that I was dumb was so ingrained in me that overcoming it has become a lifelong struggle. Being a Christian and being involved in The United Methodist Church showed me that I was capable of earning my degree. As an active youth minister, I was developing youth programs and Bible studies, writing curriculum, and speaking at youth and young adult events. All these experiences demonstrated to me that God had blessed me with the skills not only to earn my degrees but to become an ordained minister in The United Methodist Church.

Many people who have learning disabilities struggle to make it in society. They find it difficult to function. Reading instructions, street signs, restaurant menus, and other reading and writing tasks are stressful and often seem too much to overcome. The development of the personal computer changed my life and made it possible for me to function in the classroom. Taking tests and writing papers became tasks that were now manageable. However, the drive to finish my bachelor's and master's degrees came from my call to ordained ministry. The drive to accomplish what at one time seemed absolutely impossible to achieve came from God.

David James Moreno is an elder in the Rio Grande Conference. He has been director of United Methodist Campus Ministry of the Rio Grande Valley for thirteen years. His wife, Ginny, is a teacher, and their daughter, Nickie, is a college student planning to attend seminary and enter into ordained ministry.

Following God Defines My Life

Nickie Moreno

I don't know when or where God's call in my life first happened. It has always been a part of me—organically shaping the places I go, the relationships I have, the jobs I pursue. It is more a part of my identity than the way I look or where I come from. Following God is what defines my life.

While I cannot pinpoint a moment when I was called, I do have moments in my life where the direction of my call came into focus. My parents, my experiences as a youth, my opportunities to work in ministry, and the role models provided by women in ministry have all helped me to identify and clarify where God calls me.

My mom and dad introduced me to my life in ministry and are an integral part of my faith journey. I remember the Winnie the Pooh lamp, the children's Bible, and *Pockets* (a Christian magazine for children). Each night before I went to bed, my parents and I would read the Scripture of the day and pray. I remember my parents going off to church camp and retreats while I was always stuck at home. When they returned, I'd ask lots of questions: What kind of music was there? What was the theme? What did you do?

Finally, I started youth group in sixth grade at age twelve, and was able to discover what church camp and retreats were all about.

Youth ministry in the Rio Grande Conference was an important place where I encountered God's call. On April Fools' Day of my sixth-grade year, I experienced my first altar call. I had spent the weekend in worship, small groups, and making new friends. The

I had met other women in ministry, but had never been a member of a church with a female pastor.

final event on Saturday was a big worship service; everyone dressed up. The high school girls in my youth group loaned me some dressy clothes that made me feel very grown up. With this new high on maturity, I entered the service and sat next to my new best friend. She was the first friend I had whom I could talk with about God. When the preacher started the altar call, my friend and I went forward to pray together. This was not only the first altar call I experienced—the first time I didn't feel like a little kid, the first time I talked about God with a friend—it was also at this moment, on April Fools' Day, that I came to a realization that I wanted to minister to others in an ordained capacity. From that point on, at age twelve, I became vocal about my call to ministry.

When I was in eighth grade our family moved to Lewisville, Texas, in order for my dad to complete seminary. It was at First United Methodist Church in Lewisville that I went through confirmation and discovered new aspects of The United Methodist Church. I was on the district council of youth ministry and the conference council on youth ministry and attended the jurisdictional youth ministry events. I also was introduced to mission work. We traveled to different areas of the state and country to paint and rebuild homes.

Suddenly my relationship with God grew to a new level. It was not wholly internal, but external, helping people, understanding and learning about God through those different from me.

The most profound experience in Lewisville was meeting the Rev. Jill Jackson-Sears. I had met other women in ministry, but had never been a member of a church with a female pastor. Jill was our associate pastor and youth director. Jill was an encouraging and challenging role model for me when I was fifteen. Now at twenty-five, as I live through some of the same struggles she experienced and shared with me as a single woman in ministry, the lessons I learned from her then remain with me and are lived out in new ways.

In the middle of high school, my family and I left Lewisville and returned to Edinburg, Texas. I had lived in Edinburg from age four through thirteen, but this place that had once been so familiar to me now seemed foreign. Leaving the great friendships I had in Lewisville and the spiritual nurturing of my church was a painful loss. My high school in Lewisville had the latest technology and an Astroturf football stadium. In Edinburg, my high school was so poor that the entire school received free breakfast and lunch, our roof leaked, and our football team's stadium was falling apart. The move from Lewisville to the extreme poverty of the Rio Grande Valley was overwhelming.

I had so many questions for God about life, about God's nature, and about why there was so much suffering in the world around me. Struggling to make sense of my pain and confusion, I began to doubt everything I had known and experienced about God, including the existence of God. While I continued to attend church and say I was called to ministry, it felt like a complete pretense. Even though I participated in youth councils and was active at my local church, I believed that there was no God. Coupled with so much uncertainty was the feeling that there was no other job in the world I could fit into except the ministry.

It was in this conflicted state of mind that I began college. During the first month of my freshman year I became absorbed in every possible Bible study, worship service, and the first step of candidacy, the inquiry process, with my campus minister. I was desperate to discover God again, to understand who God was. Less than three weeks into my first college semester came the events of September 11, 2001. In all the Bible studies and worship services I attended after 9/11, I met with Christians who presented a vengeful, angry, and intolerant God seeking to punish the unholy and sinful.

My campus minister was different. When I was with him I was presented a grace-filled, forgiving, and loving God—a God whom I could understand, a God whose love I could feel. He questioned and challenged my doubts and by the end of the inquiring process, my faith was renewed and strengthened. The experience of 9/11 made me realize how present God was in my life, and the many ways God reached out to all people. It also ignited in me a desire to share a God of all-encompassing love with others.

Years later, in late December of 2006, I attended the Global Young People's Convocation in South Africa. It was in Johannesburg that I met United Methodists with a deep passion for social justice who were peers and mentors. In Johannesburg, we learned about what happened in South Africa during apartheid, and the way God moved through people like Nelson Mandela (whom I had idolized since I was a child). In Soweto, we saw poverty not unlike the poverty in Edinburg, Texas. This created in me the relentless desire to effect change through The United Methodist Church. I was able to help write two resolutions, "A Young People's Statement on War and Peace," and a resolution on Darfur that were both passed at General Conference 2008. Sharing God's love, bringing a message of peace, and helping those in need felt as if I had found who I was and what I was supposed to strive to be. It was as if God had revealed, uncovered me, when I'd been hiding, or denying the part of myself who wanted desperately to fight against the many injustices in our world. The Global Young People's Convocation introduced to me the enormous potential of social justice through ordained ministry. God had brought into focus a new and revolutionary call for my life. I returned from South Africa with deep passion and commitment to my new call, and have remained passionate and committed ever since, seeking ways to fulfill whom God calls me to be.

There are questions I will never be able to answer clearly or concisely, such as: When were you called? How were you called? Why were you called? God's call is organic and boundless, and it reaches out to all of creation. My life is this mystery of being called, and the pursuit of answering and following God. I expect change in my call, shifts, and new paths, and await eagerly the places God calls me to. However, God's call in my life has been aided by the people I have encountered along my journey. The Rev. Jill Jackson-Sears, the Rev. Jim Wingert, and my parents are just the beginning. There are so many people who have touched my life and helped me to accept, challenge, and listen for God, to seek the next twist or turn on the journey we take together. I know that there are more friends I will share this walk with embracing moments with God together as my friend and I did thirteen years ago.

Nickie Moreno is a student at San Antonio College and the University of Texas at San Antonio and is a candidate for ministry in the Southwest Texas Conference. She is also a member of the United Methodist Student Movement Steering Committee (2008–2010). She has a passion for social justice ministry, which was modeled for her from a young age by her father, the Rev. David James Moreno, director of the United Methodist Campus Ministry of the Rio Grande Valley.

God Has Led Me One Step at a Time

Felicia Howell LaBoy

In many ways, my call to ordained ministry and to the life of theological scholarship has been like Abraham's call to follow God without knowing where he was going, but to trust God to bless Abraham and make him a blessing and to change his name.

My call to Christian discipleship began when I was thirteen years old. My parents had gone to church when they were younger, but had later been hurt by church and were preoccupied with the challenges and opportunities of young adulthood. So they simply did not go. I began to attend church because my mother was asked if I could help care for my godmother and keep her granddaughter company. Part of the responsibility of keeping her company was going to church. It was at church that I learned the basics of the Christian faith and that God could be trusted to help in times of trouble. After I joined the church, my mother came and brought my sisters and brothers.

Although I did well at school and there was some expectation that I would attend college, what that meant and the opportunities that I could embark on as a girl were not fully known by my parents, who had never been to college and who had limited education. (My mom was a housekeeper with a high school education, and my dad was a construction worker with only a third-grade education.) Also, out of twenty-eight cousins, I would be the first girl to attend a four-year college. Consequently, I started college at nineteen.

While at college, I began to discover my gifts for leadership and business, so I changed my major from engineering to business. Because of my involvement beyond the classroom on campus, I felt the need to go to business school. I entered the Fuqua School of Business at Duke University in the fall of 1986, intent on gaining an MBA in marketing and a lucrative career in the business field.

While in school, I still attended church and prayed, occasionally. In many ways I was what Wesley calls a "practical atheist." I believed in God, called on God when I had major problems, but for the most part I lived like I didn't know God. The transforming moment in my life came right after I graduated, when I attended the funeral of a cousin who had died in a tragic accident. Because she was serving in the military at the time of her death, her friend and superior officer, who had been mentoring her in Christian discipleship, was allowed to accompany her body home and to lead a military service in her honor. Immediately after the service, this young man walked up to several of us and said, "God says he's sick and tired of you playing church. Are you going to be saved or not?" By that evening all of us made a commitment to follow the Lord wholeheartedly.

Immediately following this, I joined a Fortune 100 company in Dayton, Ohio. Although I knew that I was changed, I didn't see anyone who lived any differently from the way I had before, so I went back to my old ways. After a series of job moves, I was led back to Dayton, this time with a fiancé. After a particularly painful breakup, God again used a friend to lead me back to God, this time to a community that was serious about following God wholeheartedly, especially when it came to worship, Bible study, and meeting the needs of the marginalized.

In many ways I was what Wesley calls a "practical atheist."
I believed in God, called on God when I had major problems,
but for the most part I lived like I didn't know God.

During this time, I was also led to start a group for African-American employees at the company I where I worked. This group ushered diversity into our company. As the founding president of this organization, I explained to the group that we needed to ground our organization in God, by making prayer and spiritual growth an integral component. This was the beginning of my teaching people how to integrate faith into every aspect of their lives. Not only did I oversee our organization's advocacy of racial and gender equality, do career coaching, and initiate employee outreach to the community, I also began to serve as its spiritual leader by providing weekly "sermonettes" via e-mail, spiritual support to individuals, and weekly Bible study, as well as regular corporate and private prayer sessions with other colleagues.

It was at this time that God called me to ordained ministry, which I immediately protested. I felt that what I did as president of

God Calls Abraham

Now the LORD said to Abram, "Go from your country and your kindred and your father's house to the land that I will show you. I will make of you a great nation, and I will bless you, and make your name great, so that you will be a blessing. I will bless those who bless you, and the one who curses you I will curse; and in you all the families of the earth shall be blessed."

So Abram went, as the LORD had told him; and Lot went with him. Abram was seventy-five years old when he departed from Haran. Abram took his wife Sarai and his brother's son Lot, and all the possessions that they had gathered, and the persons whom they had acquired in Haran; and they set forth to go to the land of Canaan. When they had come to the land of Canaan, Abram passed through the land to the place at Shechem, to the oak of Moreh. At that time the Canaanites were in the land. Then the LORD appeared to Abram, and said, "To your offspring I will give this land." So he built there an altar to the LORD, who had appeared to him. From there he moved on to the hill country on the east of Bethel, and pitched his tent, with Bethel on the west and Ai on the east; and there he built an altar to the LORD and invoked the name of the LORD. And Abram journeyed on by stages toward the Negeb.

(Genesis 12:1-9)

our employees' organization, which was in addition to my regular job, was simply my Christian duty, not an indication I was called to ordained ministry. I was led to meet with an elder at my church who confirmed that what I had done as president was indeed pastoral ministry and that I was being called. Thus, as I prayed more about my calling, God led me to give up the presidency of the organization. Interestingly enough, when I stopped serving as president, the members asked me to take on as a full-time role the spiritual leadership of the group. However, there was still this hunger in me to learn more about the things of God and God's people.

Still running from my call to ministry, I thought that I could pursue interests in a Ph.D. in intercultural relations or perhaps attend Bible college. While attending Bible college, the Lord again spoke to me about leaving my job and going into ministry full time. After I completed Bible college, I was laid off from my job and thus, my ministry at work. After starting a business to help better equip smaller ministries and nonprofits, God reminded me of my calling to ordained ministry and through a series of events and people, led me to Garrett-Evangelical Theological Seminary.

I must admit that I was quite angry. After all, I didn't feel that I was "good enough" (I didn't pray enough, have faith enough, and behave well enough to be a pastor). But through prayer, through students and faculty at the seminary, God kept confirming my call and leading me. The summer after my first semester God impressed upon me the need to participate in a special program for women in ministry. At this program I interned at Southlawn United Methodist Church in Chicago and at the General Board of Pension and Health Benefits. It was at Southlawn that I was "forced" to accept my pastoral identity by "robing up" and being acknowledged as a member of the pastoral staff.

Upon leaving Southlawn I completed my Field Education work at West Ridge United Methodist Church in Chicago where I had to take on more pastoral responsibilities. In fact, when the pastor announced his retirement, it was the congregation who recognized my pastoral gifts and requested that I become their senior pastor.

This was not to be and God led me to Mandell United Methodist Church, also in Chicago, where I served as the senior pastor while completing my M.Div. While at Mandell, God began to impress upon me that I was called not only to ordained ministry but also to academic theological scholarship and teaching.

In the fall of 2002, just a couple of short weeks after my wedding and honeymoon, and in the midst of serving as pastor at the congregation at Mandell, I began my Ph.D. in theology, history, and economics, with a particular interest and emphasis on church-based community and economic development in the black church. Again, timid, sure that I couldn't do this, I stepped out and God sent others like the mentors of the United Methodist Women of Color Scholars program, especially Angella Current-Felder, Drs. Karen Collier, Rosetta Ross, Rita Nakashima Brock, and Jung Ha Kim; faculty at Garrett-Evangelical like Drs. Linda Thomas, Henry Young, Larry Murphy, Ken Vaux, and Steve Long; pastors like Rev. Dr. Tracy Smith Malone and Rev. Dr. Pamela Lightsey; and a host of family and friends, especially my husband, Adrian, who believed in me and encouraged my gifts for theological scholarship.

I am happy to report that I am in the process of completing what I thought I could never do—my dissertation titled *Personal and Social Holiness: The Sacraments and the Mandate for Christian Community and Economic Development for the Black Church.*

It has been thirteen years since God called me, ten years since I moved to Chicago to prepare for that calling, and eight years since I have served officially as a pastor. I've tried to follow that calling— kicking, screaming, crying, laughing, feeling amazed, and rejoicing at all that God has done and how God has led me one step at a time in ways I would have never thought possible or even imagined. Like Abraham, I have found that God has not only blessed me and made me a blessing but that God has changed my name—to pastor and scholar—just as God promised.

Felicia Howell LaBoy is an elder in full connection with the Northern Illinois Conference and the senior pastor at Maple Park United Methodist Church. She is completing her Ph.D. at Garrett-Evangelical Theological Seminary in theology, ethics, and economics with an emphasis in Christian Community and Economic Development as a means to restore spiritual, moral, and economic vitality to inner-city neighborhoods. She is married to Adrian LaBoy. They are the proud grandparents of eleven grandchildren and currently reside in Blue Island, Illinois.

God Planted Seeds for My Journey of Faith

Justin Halbersma

If I were to paint a picture of my call to ministry, it would look like this: a young boy being led down a path by his family. His family members would continue to push him along the path and tell him to go on ahead of them, but the boy would always hesitate. The boy knew that his family members could see where the path led, but it was as if he didn't have the binoculars to see as far as they could. However, the boy trusted that they knew where he was supposed to venture, and so he continued to follow where they led. The boy got so caught up traveling on the path and listening to his family as they journeyed along that he didn't even pay attention to the horizon anymore.

Then one day the boy awoke and started down the path and things looked different. He could see farther than ever before and what he saw was beautiful. He could tell that this beauty in the distance was where he was meant to travel to and he turned to his family and said, "I see. I see the path that is meant for me. Thank you for leading me here. I can see now that it is mine." Then the boy took off to enjoy the beauty that called him like a siren song.

That simple narrative describes my call journey. I am currently a provisional member working toward elder's orders in the Minnesota Annual Conference. I am twenty-eight years old and have been married six years to my wife, Stacy. We have an energetic three-year-old boy named Micah who fills our days with laughter and challenges.

This is who I am now: a son of God journeying down the path that God sets before me. But the path was not always clear to me internally.

I grew up in a single-parent household, just my mother and me. We moved many times when I was younger, as my mother went from job to job. But there were always two constants in my life: my mother's family and the church. Growing up, I was a part of many faith communities from the Christian Missionary Alliance Church all the way to my current home in The United Methodist Church. My call story is littered with individuals and instances where I was told or shown externally that God was calling me into the ministry. (Think about the boy traveling down the path with his family but unable to see the beauty far off that they could see was meant for him.)

The first instance of external recognition came when I was in eighth grade. My mother and I had attended Faith Community Reformed Church in Alexandria, Minnesota, since I was in first grade. However, since second grade we had lived in Sauk Centre, Minnesota, about twenty-five minutes away from Alexandria. In my elementary years, it wasn't that big a deal, but when I reached junior high I began to become an outsider among the church youth, because they saw one another daily while I only saw them once or twice in any given week.

There came a point in time when I asked my mother if I could go to the United Methodist church in Sauk Centre because so many of my friends and my choir director went there. My mother said yes, and so I found a new church home, but when I went to transfer my membership, Faith Community Reformed Church would not release me until the pastor and an elder came to speak to me. I was annoyed as a young teenager because I just wanted to be in The United Methodist Church and couldn't understand why they wouldn't let me. Well, one Saturday the pastor and the elder came and spoke to my mother and me. They shared with us how they didn't want me to leave the church because they felt I was a leader for the youth in

The experience of working in the church and with the staff gave me that internal heart recognition that this was where I was meant to be.

the church. At the time I didn't fully understand the gravity of that moment because I just wanted to be United Methodist, but in that moment a seed was planted in my mind.

Five years later, when I was at Northwestern College in Orange City, Iowa, there was another instance. (Remember the boy ventured down the path and got caught up with where his family was leading him.) I was working toward my religion degree because, in my mind, I recognized that the church saw something in me as a leader. This sentiment was again affirmed when the resident director of my dorm spoke to me about becoming a resident assistant because he could see that I was meant to be a leader to the others in my dorm. At the time I just thought it was awesome that the coolest resident director on campus wanted me to work for him as a resident assistant.

Who Are Elders?

Elders are persons called by God, authorized by the church, and ordained by a bishop to a lifetime ministry of Word, Sacrament, Order, and Service.

What Does a Ministry of Word, Sacrament, Order, and Service Mean?

Like all baptized Christians, elders are committed to a lifetime of service, although this service most often manifests itself in different ways from that of deacons or the laity. The elder embodies, or brings to life, Christ's teachings in servant ministries and servant leadership. The elder gives pastoral leadership in ordering the life of the congregation for service.

Elders devote themselves to the ministry of the Word, which includes primary responsibility for preaching and teaching the Word of God.

The unique calling of elders is pastoral oversight for the ordering of the church. They also have primary responsibility for administering the sacraments of baptism and Holy Communion. Because elders have been ordained to ordering the ministry of the church and administering church policies through the *Discipline*, bishops and district superintendents are chosen from ordained elders.

Where Do Elders Serve?

For most elders, their calling will be lived out as pastors in local congregations. However, elders are not restricted to local

Justin Halbersma serves Holy Communion at Chatfield United Methodist Church in Chatfield, Minnesota.

church service and may be appointed to extension ministries outside of the church walls.

How Do Elders Find Work?

Elders make a commitment to full-time service under the authority of a bishop, willing to serve wherever the bishop appoints. Elders serve continually and are assigned annually by the bishop to the same or a different appointment.

But again a seed was planted in my mind. This was further evidence to my analytical mind that God had called me to something. (Remember again the boy getting caught up in the journey.)

At this point in my life I could mentally recognize that God had called me into ministry, but in my heart I didn't have that affirmation. I was still unsure. (Relating my experience to the story of John Wesley, my heart had not yet become "strangely warmed.")

Well, I had met Stacy my freshman year and things had progressed to engagement and then marriage when I graduated from Northwestern. But she had transferred to Southwest State University in Marshall, Minnesota, our sophomore year so I couldn't head straight off to seminary like I had planned. I moved to Marshall after the wedding and began to look for jobs. In 2002 the economy was in a downturn, and having a religion major didn't get you many interviews in the world of business. Luckily, the fact that I was in accelerated math in high school landed me a job as an inventory control clerk at a manufacturing plant. (I guess being able to do calculus has to mean you are able to count inventory.)

I was happy to have a job and was excited to be married to Stacy, but two months into the job I started to realize something: I missed the church. I could tell that I didn't belong behind a counter counting magnetic cores. My home was the church and so I began to look for jobs that might be open that would allow me to work with youth in the churches around Marshall. I ended up as the youth director at Wesley United Methodist Church in Marshall. It was there in my year-and-a-half of youth ministry that my heart was warmed and I finally internally felt the call. The experience of working in the church and with the staff gave me that internal heart recognition that this was where I was meant to be. So after my wife graduated we headed off to Durham, North Carolina, so I could attend Duke Divinity School.

It was at Duke that I finally had that full experience and calmness that comes with knowing one is headed on the right path.

(Think about the boy now being able to see the far-off beauty and knowing that is where he was meant to be.) The community at Duke helped me forge my identity as someone called into ministry, but more important, they helped me see the beauty that lay ahead. Duke was a place for me where my newly affirmed inner call was able to be developed and affirmed in new ministry contexts and with new relationships with others on the same journey.

Now I find myself in Chatfield, Minnesota, serving a rural church. It is one stop along the path as I continue to journey where God is leading, but now I journey not just intellectually knowing God has called me. I now journey with a calming spiritual sense that God is using me in ways I could never have imagined, and I see the beauty that lies ahead. This boy is thankful for his family within the church who helped him externally recognize the call and continued to guide him down the path until internally he could recognize it for himself.

It is my hope that as you have read my call to ministry that you have been able to see how God is calling you. I pray that your life is blessed with a community to support you and journey with you as that call is nurtured.

Justin Halbersma is a provisional member, working toward elder's orders in the Minnesota Annual Conference. He serves Central United Methodist Church in Winona, Minnesota, as an associate pastor in charge of outreach to young adults and young families and is also a part-time campus minister at Winona State University.

I Am the Church, Too, and I'll Do Something Different

Jennifer L. Battiest

As a child, I loved going to church. I grew up in a small Native American United Methodist church of thirty or forty members; most of the church members were also family members. The services were in the Choctaw language, and we had Sunday morning, Sunday night, and Wednesday night services. Every fifth Sunday, we had all-day services and singing. There was even a hog-killing cabin so there would be fresh meat.

At age four, I decided to be a missionary when I grew up. In my four-year-old mind, a missionary was simply one who worked with the church. When I got older and learned about what some missionaries, some churches, and the government did to Native people, I was embarrassed by my childhood ambition.

I went to college depressed because while I was pretty good at most everything, I had no passion for any particular subject. I drifted through one major after another. I could feel God starting to try to woo me. I said no thanks.

But I began to see something in the eyes of the people around me. At clubs, at powwows, at an Indian protest, I saw this emptiness, this deadness, in the eyes of some Native people around me. It scared me, and I stopped going to those places. Then, on Sunday morning at the church I attended, I saw it in the eyes of church people. I asked God what was wrong with them. God asked if I would help them. Because I could feel what God was also asking me to do, I asked, "Why would anyone listen to me anyway?" I got no answer, so I wrestled with my desire to be left alone and with my conscience.

If God thought I could help people who were hurting, and I could see them hurting, why wouldn't I do something to help ease that pain? After a couple of weeks, worn out and reluctant, I told God that if I could really be of help, if I was told what to do and what to say, if what I did would help those people stop hurting, then yes, I would go.

But it wasn't until seminary that I got mad. Sitting in church history class, I listened to stories of the removal of Native Americans to reservations and of slavery and the church's role in all of it. I was mad and sick listening to the church's bloody history. I read a story of a Jewish man who was angry at God about the Holocaust. He said, "Even God cannot undo the past," and I agreed with him. Even God could not undo what had been done. And I wrestled with that because I knew that God had called me.

I told God that I wasn't going to go back home to Oklahoma, back to the Oklahoma Indian Missionary Conference, as an agent of the institutional church that to this day doesn't seem to want to understand racism, or study racism, or even consider the possibility that racism still exists. I was not going back and tell Native people to forgive the church. How was I supposed to tell them to forgive when I couldn't? And I would not forgive what the church had done.

I went to Africa, to Ghana, for my cross-cultural credits at Drew Theological School. We visited two of twenty-four slave castles. We were led from room to room, led into the almost airless dungeons underground. The tour guide talked about the atrocities that happened there and in the surrounding village of El Mina. He said people don't remember what happened there, and live their lives with no memory of the horror.

My first thought on hearing this was, "Oh, I understand that. What happened here was so bad, it was so horrendous that nothing was ever going to put it right, to fix it, and to ensure no one tries to fix it, we will tell people we do not remember." I don't know if that is what they thought. Maybe they really just forgot. But as I walked back to our tour bus, looking at the faces of the young people trying to sell us things, coming from a background of cultural collective memory, I don't think they have forgotten.

I came back to the United States wrapped up in thoughts of the people of El Mina and about Native people all trapped in some sort of loop of pain and horror that generation after generation is forced to live out. Something had to be done, but I refused to forgive.

I graduated, and despite my best effort and considerable willpower, I ended up on the ordination track with two churches in Oklahoma. The first church offered to me was a church that had dwindled down to two faithful little girls. I said no, but I remembered how I loved going to church so I went back and said yes. In the back of my mind I began thinking of the things the church had gotten wrong with Indian people. I promised myself that this church will never tell these kids that they are not welcome. They will learn about a God who loves every cultural bit of them. They will hear that their culture, their language, and their brown skin are gifts from God. The church is not perfect, but I am the church too, and I will change what it means in the lives of these little kids. As long as I am here, the church will not hurt them.

Later, I moved to Clinton Indian United Methodist Church in the middle of a Cheyenne/Arapaho community of Clinton, Oklahoma. My kids are mostly Cheyenne/Arapaho. I went from two children to about fifteen and about thirty on holidays. Most of the kids live within a

Native American Scholarships

Since 1872, The United Methodist Church has provided financial assistance to its members interested in pursuing their vocational calling and obtaining an undergraduate degree or attending seminary. Native American students who are members of The United Methodist Church are eligible for many scholarships, beginning with the general United Methodist Student Loans and Scholarships Programs, which have helped more than 4,000 United Methodist students each year have access to a college or university of their choice because of the church's financial support.

In addition, Native American undergraduates are eligible for other scholarships, including the Ethnic Minority Scholarship, the HANA Scholarship, and the Reverend Dr. Karen Layman Gift of Hope Scholarship.

Seminary students can apply for the Native American Seminary Award, while graduate students are eligible for the Women of Color Scholars Program, the Georgia Harkness Scholarship, and the Dempster Fellowship.

To learn more, visit www.gbhem.org/loansandscholarships.

three-block radius of the church and they just show up, with their parents. The Cheyenne and Arapaho people are the people of the Sand Creek Massacre. On November 29, 1864, soldiers from the U.S. military, led by Col. John Chivington, who was also a Methodist minister, attacked a peaceful encampment of Cheyenne and Arapaho along Sand Creek. More than 150 Indians were killed in the attack, most of whom were women, children, or elderly. There is a pastor in the Oklahoma Missionary Indian Conference whose great-great-grandparents escaped the Sand Creek massacre, only to be killed four years later at the Massacre of the Washita in 1868. The site of this massacre is just northwest of my church.

The church and the government's involvement in the removal, in the boarding schools, in the relocation acts, in trying to kill the

Indian and save the man, well, none of these has a good reputation in Oklahoma. I believe this is why adults aren't coming to the church. They are also Sun Dance ceremonial people, and even the Indian churches haven't always been supportive of this culture. Some of our Indian churches are still living out the harsh rules and regulations of the missionaries who taught them to think Native culture is wrong.

But I like to think that what I am doing with the kids, my determination that they learn of a God who thinks they are special and extraordinary, is helping undo some of the past.

I think of what that Jewish man said about even God not being able to undo the past. I had agreed with him at the time, but now I think it's possible to break the hold the past can have on a person. By breaking the hold the past has on you, you are then able to change the trajectory of where you are heading.

Working with the children helped change the trajectory of where that church was headed. It was to be closed down, but now it is a church and community center under the General Board of Global Ministries program. I like to think it's helping change the trajectory of where the children are headed, just as it helped change the trajectory of where I was headed.

Because in the midst of it all, I think I figured out how to forgive the church. To be honest, I was disappointed when I realized I could forgive, because that is not what I intended to do. But my feeling of not being able to forgive is not there anymore; it's gone. What helped it go was that I keep thinking, "I am the church, too, and I'll do something different."

I achieved my four-year-old dream. I am a church and community worker, a missionary, and I am no longer embarrassed by those roles.

Jennifer L. Battiest is a church and community worker through the United Methodist General Board of Global Ministries and a provisional elder in the Oklahoma Indian Missionary Conference.

In Countless Ways, God Manages to Find the Way In

Jeremy Wester

I really couldn't tell you the first time I felt God knocking on the door to my heart. I just know that as I look back I can see the countless ways God has managed to find his way in. I've never seen the heavens part, time has never stood still on my behalf, and I certainly don't expect to see the Spirit of God descend like a dove over me any time soon. In fact, there's nothing grand or epic about my story at all, just a lot of little things that have come together in a big way to make me the person that I am today.

I was born into a United Methodist family, and I don't just mean we went to the local United Methodist church. One of my great-grandfathers was a circuit-riding preacher many years ago. I don't know much about the rest of his generation, but both sets of grandparents are long-time Methodists and my parents were both active lay members of the church. They met at the Wesley Foundation at Texas A&M during college and my mom was even the youth director at my church when I started junior high. I guess you could say church has been in my blood since birth.

Up until college, Sunday morning attendance was more of an expectation than an option. In my family, you were in church unless you were sick or out of town, and there was an unwritten rule that youth group events would be funded over any other form of entertainment. Having this background, I have always been at home in

In fact, there's nothing grand or epic about my story at all, just a lot of little things that have come together in a big way to make me the person that I am today.

the church and never felt any desire to leave. I even took the opportunity as a young boy to make friends with my pastor on the summer days that my mom would have to work and I was too young to stay home alone. I remember times when I would sit in the back of the huge sanctuary staring at a beautiful stained glass portrait of Jesus reaching down toward two of his followers. To this day, I don't really know the full symbolism of the window, but I remember the amazing feeling it gave me to sit in that holy place and gaze upon the face of our Lord. Of course, I didn't have much understanding at the time of what gave me those feelings, I just knew on some level that I was at home in the presence of God.

It wasn't until I was a sophomore in high school that I came to know the fullness of God's presence in my heart. As I said in the beginning, I really couldn't tell you the first time God began to knock on the door to my heart, but I can tell you with absolute certainty about the first time God tore down every wall to my heart and filled me completely with God's love. My family had moved to Pflugerville, Texas, that summer and by January I was on a midwinter retreat with a bunch of people that I barely knew. Don't get me wrong, I really liked the youth group and the youth director had a profound influence on my life; it just takes me a while to get comfortable with people.

So there I was on the retreat, still getting to know my own youth group and suddenly plunged into a group of several hundred unfamiliar faces. In the midst of my uneasiness and fear, I was given a time to sit and listen for the voice of God. During that time, my youth director came over, laid hands on my shoulders, and began to pray. As he finished praying, something happened to me that I can't even begin to put into words. I have never been at such a loss for words and understanding. The strange thing was for the first time in my life everything made sense. I had always believed in and followed God, but in that moment things clicked like the last piece of the puzzle was finally in place.

The overwhelming feeling of God's presence gave me a profound look into the reality and meaning of being a child of the risen Lord and a look into the heart of God. In a moment that would probably mean nothing to the rest of the world, I was able to experience the power and call of God in a tangible way. Even as a child I knew on some level that I could never be happy without sharing the power of Christ with everyone I met. Things had just become a little more concrete in that moment and I began to accept my call into ordained ministry.

I certainly had not committed to the vocation yet. I wasn't exactly running from the path God had laid out for me, but I was definitely taking some back roads. I went to college as a physics major because I loved math and science and figured I would change the world by proving Einstein wrong and determining an entirely new scientific view of the world. Those dreams quickly faded, however, as I realized again and again that I could never really enjoy

United Methodist Seminaries

In Romans 10:14, Paul asked the questions that have echoed in the call heard by men and women throughout the centuries: How will they believe if they have not heard? How will they hear without a preacher? How can they preach unless they are sent?

To that we might add, "How will they be sent if they are not trained for ministry?" A strong commitment to the training and formation for those who seek to serve Jesus Christ undergirds the ordained ministry of The United Methodist Church.

Through the thirteen United Methodist seminaries, the church is forming, shaping, and training men and women for a variety of Christian ministries. These excellent schools provide the foundation for those who have responded to God's call so that they might effectively live out their particular vocation.

As you prayerfully consider God's call in your life, we invite you to consider one of these schools for your seminary training. Visit the campuses and talk with the students and faculty. You can also find out more information about these campuses and other United Methodist–related institutions at our Web site: www.gbhem.org.

May God bless you as you prepare to serve the church and the world in the name of Jesus Christ.

The Reverend Mary Ann Moman
Associate General Secretary
Division of Ordained Ministry
General Board of Higher Education and Ministry

a vocation outside the ministry. I still love math and science, but I decided to put that on the back burner for a time and became a philosophy major, still not fully committed to the idea of becoming a pastor, but at least willing to get a degree that would prepare me for the types of things I would learn in seminary, should I choose to attend.

College was again a time of many small things coming together to help solidify my call into ordained ministry. It took a while for me to find my church home. I don't know if it was a subconscious desire to look beyond The United Methodist Church or just a case of being lazy, but I applied for and got into a Christian leadership organization at Texas A&M and, for my freshman year, treated it like my church home. It was what I would call a non-denominational Southern Baptist organization, as are many college ministries in College Station. I don't really have anything against such ministries, except to say that they aren't where I belong. It was, however, a good experiment in finding where I fit into the church and gave me greater clarity in knowing that The United Methodist Church is where I belong. Still, I had to start all over finding a church home when my freshman year ended.

I began by checking out the Wesley Foundation where my parents had met so many years before, figuring that it couldn't be a bad place to start since it had a big hand in my being on this earth in the first place. Little did I know at the time that it would become my home for the next three years and it would be the place where God finally got control of my whole self, vocation and all. The campus minister, Max Mertz, pretty quickly began to push me toward ordination. After contemplating my calling and taking the back roads for so long, I finally decided to get on the ordination track and see where God might take me.

I read all the books and met with Max countless times. I got more involved with Wesley than I ever thought possible, easily spending eight or more hours a day with my Christian family and taking various leadership roles. I went on all the retreats and even

Jeremy Wester and other members of the Texas A&M Wesley Foundation at work on a Hurricane Rita recovery mission trip during spring break 2006.

joined the conference Board of Higher Education and Campus Ministry, which oversees the operations and budgets of all Wesley Foundations in the Texas Annual Conference. Through all of these experiences, I continued to feel right at home learning what it really meant to submit to God in service of the church. I served as a pastoral intern for the conference during the summer after graduating college and am presently beginning my master of divinity at Duke Divinity School as a certified candidate for ministry with the Texas Annual Conference.

To this day God continues to knock on the door to my heart and ensure I'm traveling God's path for my life. As I look back I can see so many little blessings that God has poured out on me to make sure I would find my home in ministry for God. I was given a loving family to instill in me the value of the church. I was blessed beyond measure to meet my fiancée at the Wesley Foundation, just like my parents met years ago. I found friendships in Christian community during youth and college and have been given countless opportunities to live in and serve the body of Christ. God still hasn't parted a sea for me and I don't reckon I'll be able to walk on water any time soon, but I can rest easy in my calling knowing that the presence and love of Christ will be with me throughout the rest of the ordination process and throughout my life, gently nudging me along in my life's journey closer to God.

Jeremy Wester is a student at Duke Divinity School and a certified candidate for ministry in the Texas Annual Conference.

I Wanted God to Give Me a Samuel-like Experience

Kimberly Hall

J amaica is where I first encountered God's nudge leading me in the direction of ordained ministry. Although I was raised and baptized in the church, the notion of seeking the vocation of clergy was far from my dreams for my life. I was a graduate student at Howard University majoring in film/scriptwriting, pursuing a career as a television producer. It was at Howard that I met the Reverend Lillian Smith. She was the chaplain at the Wesley Foundation and was one of the women I interviewed for a mini-documentary video I was producing about women in ministry. After my project was completed, she invited me to join her and other students from Howard and Texas A&M on a mission trip to the small Caribbean island of Jamaica. After much contemplation, I said yes.

One day as we worked with the local Methodist community to construct the foundation of a building, I was approached by the

Rev. Kenneth Green, a campus minister from Texas Southern University. He was noticeably taller than I with a booming voice and a slight Southern drawl. He pulled me aside, pointed his finger directly in my face, and said, "Girl, you've got something on you. You goin' to be a preacher." I said, "No, I am not." He then laughed a deep-throated laugh.

Throughout the week, Rev. Green continued to repeat what he was discerning as a call on my life. Every time he mentioned it, I rejected it. The word *no* seemed to stir up in him an eruption of laughter. Strangely, however, I was flattered by the idea even as it horrified me. Before we parted, he looked me in my eyes and said, "Kim, when you have your first initial sermon, give me a call." In my heart, I said, "That's never going to happen." But I politely nodded and we went our separate ways.

A few months after the mission trip, I accepted a position in Durham, North Carolina, as a television production specialist. The year was 1997 and I was thrilled to get my toe in the door as I ambitiously sought a career in the field of television. One of my primary responsibilities was to teach people in the community the elements of production that included camera work, lighting, and editing. In many of the classes I led, I encountered several pastors. Some of them also thought they discerned the call on me toward the path of ministry. But I wasn't convinced. I thought if God wants me, God has to call me.

Over time, I began to feel a sense of restlessness, which I couldn't understand. I was in a job that was satisfying. But the restlessness wouldn't go away. It gnawed at me until I finally prayed and said, "God, if you want me to go into the ministry, I want a Samuel-like experience." Samuel was the boy-child who served under Eli the priest. Samuel had an encounter with God in the wee hours of the morning. Little did I realize when praying this prayer that God would have a similar surprise for me.

In the spring of 1999, like Samuel, I, too, had a series of middle-of-the-night wake-up calls. It always happened around

3 a.m. when I would wake from a sound sleep. I secretly knew in my heart that God wanted to speak with me. I was afraid, because I felt that if I sat up to listen, God would call me into the ministry and I simply didn't want that. So, instead of listening, I buried and hid myself under the covers of my bed. In retrospect, I realize that I was running away.

God has a way of patiently catching up with us. Weeks later, I attended an evening Palm Sunday service in a United Methodist church. There was a woman scheduled to preach. I can't recall her name, but I remember her sermon title. It was, "What Is Your Divine Calling?" As she boldly proclaimed God's word, I felt as though she was speaking directly to me. My heart quickened and I began to squirm in the pew. I later learned that this was not the sermon that she had initially prepared. She told me that when she stood up to preach, the Holy Spirit told her to change her sermon. That night I went to bed, and was aroused again at 3 a.m.

Instead of ignoring it, this time I sat upright in my bed and I began worshiping God. "Hallelujah, praise the Lord, thank you, Jesus," I said. I repeated this act of worship for a long time. While in the midst of praising God, I began to speak in tongues. This was totally unfamiliar to me. The church that I grew up in was very traditional and I wasn't exposed to anything like this. But here I was sitting upright in my bed with this strange language coming out of my mouth that I didn't understand. I recall reaching for my throat and trying to say something audible but every time I would try to say something in English the language got stronger and wouldn't let me go. I had no control.

It was as though God had shut off my vocal cords and was saying to me, "If you want something dramatic, I will give you something dramatic." But as the language continued, I became deathly afraid. And when I got to the point where I didn't think I could handle it anymore, the strange language stopped just as suddenly as it started. I then took my Bible and I opened it randomly and one of the many Scriptures that spoke to me was the passage in Isaiah where it reads in part, "The spirit of the Lord GOD is upon me, because the LORD has anointed me; he has sent me to bring good news to the oppressed, to bind up the brokenhearted, to proclaim liberty to the captives, and release to the prisoners" (Isaiah 61:1). On March 30, 1999, I said, "Yes, Lord, I'll go." I immediately felt the restlessness leave my body and the peace of God fill my very soul. It is indescribable what I felt in that early morning hour. But I knew in my heart that I had made the right decision.

Later that morning, I made a call to the Reverend Kenneth Green. I smiled as I began to speak the words "You were right."

Kimberly Hall is an elder in the Baltimore-Washington Conference and lead pastor of Epworth United Methodist Church in Cockeysville, Maryland.

God Calls Samuel

Now the boy Samuel was ministering to the LORD under Eli. The word of the LORD was rare in those days; visions were not widespread.

At that time Eli, whose eyesight had begun to grow dim so that he could not see, was lying down in his room; the lamp of God had not yet gone out, and Samuel was lying down in the temple of the LORD, where the ark of God was. Then the LORD called, "Samuel! Samuel!" and he said, "Here I am!" and ran to Eli, and said, "Here I am, for you called me." But he said, "I did not call; lie down again." So he went and lay down. The LORD called again, "Samuel!" Samuel got up and went to Eli, and said, "Here I am, for you called me." But he said, "I did not call, my son; lie down again." Now

Samuel did not yet know the LORD, and the word of the LORD had not yet been revealed to him. The LORD called Samuel again, a third time. And he got up and went to Eli, and said, "Here I am, for you called me." Then Eli perceived that the LORD was calling the boy. Therefore Eli said to Samuel, "Go, lie down; and if he calls you, you shall say, 'Speak, LORD, for your servant is listening.'" So Samuel went and lay down in his place.

Now the LORD came and stood there, calling as before, "Samuel! Samuel!" And Samuel said, "Speak, for your servant is listening." Then the LORD said to Samuel, "See, I am about to do something in Israel that will make both ears of anyone who hears of it tingle. On that day I will fulfill against Eli all that I have spoken concerning his house, from beginning to end. For I have told him that I am about to punish his house forever, for the iniquity that he knew, because his sons were blaspheming God, and he did not restrain them. Therefore I swear to the house of Eli that the iniquity of Eli's house shall not be expiated by sacrifice or offering forever."

Samuel lay there until morning; then he opened the doors of the house of the LORD. Samuel was afraid to tell the vision to Eli. But Eli called Samuel and said, "Samuel, my son." He said, "Here I am." Eli said, "What was it that he told you? Do not hide it from me. May God do so to you and more also, if you hide anything from me of all that he told you." So Samuel told him everything and hid nothing from him. Then he said, "It is the LORD; let him do what seems good to him."

As Samuel grew up, the LORD was with him and let none of his words fall to the ground. And all Israel from Dan to Beer-sheba knew that Samuel was a trustworthy prophet of the LORD. The LORD continued to appear at Shiloh, for the LORD revealed himself to Samuel at Shiloh by the word of the LORD. And the word of Samuel came to all Israel. (1 Samuel 3:1-19)

Here I Am Lord, Looking Forward With Faith

Robert Aaron Perales

I can remember the calming, yet exciting pulse of the Holy Spirit in the tabernacle atop the mountains in New Mexico. My knees were trembling, my eyes were damp, and I could truly feel the urgency of God's hand upon me. As I stood up and began the short walk to the back of the tabernacle, up the stairs, and into the room, I was gripped with a sense of excitement and certainty about God's calling for my life.

The will that God placed upon me came while I was at my first Rio Grande Conference camp in Sacramento, New Mexico. Throughout that week, I had been taking a class, as it happened, about answering God's call. As one would expect, we covered nearly every possible calling offered in The United Methodist Church. I had never really envisioned myself as a pastor; at the time I had only been a Christian for a little more than eighteen months. I was quite proficient in music and was mildly considering a career something along the lines of a worship director. The idea of standing behind a pulpit, sitting at the head of an administrative meeting, and helping the people of God with their various personal problems seemed hardly suited for me. However, on one of my last days at camp, the time came for those who felt a pull toward ordained ministry to come forward.

I cannot accurately put into words my experience. I found myself halfway up the stairs that led to the directed room when I realized where I was. To this day, I do not remember getting up from my chair and taking the initial steps that have placed me on the path

I now realize that God truly knows us all; only God knows exactly how to impact our lives in the right way so as to impart the realization of God's Divine Will.

that I now find myself. At the time, I really wasn't sure what to make of this. As time has passed, I have spent countless hours in deep meditation about this. I now realize that God truly knows us all; only God knows exactly how to impact our lives in the right way so as to impart the realization of God's Divine Will.

As I already stated, this was far from any idea of my intended goals. As I continued on with my life, I put my faith in God that this is what God wanted me to do. I began preparing sermons, opening myself to opportunities to give spiritual counsel, and began more in-depth personal Bible studies. As I progressed down this path, I really felt at peace and shared a connection with God that I never experienced before. Soon thereafter, I felt a strong urge to give my first sermon. I was seventeen years old and I was preaching to my home church—I had never felt such a mixture of fear and nervousness in my life. But, as soon as I opened my mouth I felt a calm that can only be explained by the presence of the Holy Spirit. There were times when I couldn't feel myself present or hear myself speaking; the tremendous power that overtook me on that day was truly pure and holy.

It has been nearly three years since that morning and yet the memory is as fresh as yesterday. With faith, I have continued down this road laid out for me by God and I have yet to face an obstacle that could not be overcome through the trust and grace of God.

Following my high school graduation, I enrolled at Southern Arkansas University (SAU), where my calling truly solidified. I no longer had the comfort of the presence of people my own color; I was in uncharted territory. As God so often does, though, he opened a door for me. It was at the Wesley Foundation on the campus of SAU that I found my first ministry. In truth, proclaiming the Word to people whom I had not known my whole life, who were far from my own personal experience, truly put into perspective the calling that God had placed upon me. I was, and always will be, a minister and pastor to the people of God. In my time spent at SAU, I was able to give more sermons than I can count, and impact lives that only through the omnipotence of the Father could have allowed. Sadly, the ministry that I had become a part of was short-lived and after a mere ten months, I departed.

Since then, my time has been spent at Southern Methodist University (SMU) in Dallas, the place where I really felt that God wanted me. Since my arrival, I have not been able to do nearly as much preaching as I had done at SAU, but I have gained an immense knowledge, both academically and spiritually, that has truthfully built my character and reliance on God. In retrospect, I have realized why God has placed me at SMU.

Through the people whom God has placed in contact with me, I have gained an understanding of not only counseling but of God's people that I have never experienced anywhere else. While it may

ExploreCalling.org Helps Examine Calling

ExploreCalling.org invites people to consider God's call in their lives, provides answers to questions about United Methodist candidacy and ministry, and enables ongoing conversations that will "bridge" ministry candidates from one phase of vocational exploration to the next.

The Web site developed by the General Board of Higher Education and Ministry will help youth, college students, seminary students, and young adults who are considering how God is calling them and how they can serve in the UMC—either as laypeople or as clergy. Links to United Methodist colleges, universities, and seminaries are there, as well as information about scholarships available to United Methodist students. Other new resources are high-lighted as well.

Visitors to the site may sign up to receive e-newsletters with updated information and highlighted features.

seem strange, I had never sincerely appreciated the responsibility that came with my calling. Because of the many people whom God has placed in front of me, both as tests and faith-builders, the sheer magnitude that I can carry through God's power has been realized; I am now aware of the impact that my words, beliefs, and especially actions have on his people. I have many years left at SMU and can only continue to persevere and look forward to the influences that God will place in my mind and heart.

The presence of God is something that is truly incomparable to any other experience that we can have on earth. By accepting the truth of Jesus Christ in my life, I was given an opportunity to be a part of something unearthly; by choosing to follow the calling that God created me for, I grasped that opportunity. The calling God sent to me cannot simply be described as a moment in my life; it is a decision that, since its inception, has continually directed and altered my life.

Robert Aaron Perales grew up in the Rio Grande Valley of South Texas. Currently, he is a senior religious studies major at Southern Methodist University in Dallas. Following his graduation in May 2009, he plans to pursue a masters of divinity at SMU's Perkins School of Theology.

God's Call Can Come in Unexpected Places

Elonda Clay

don't have a dramatic, heroic story about my call. There was no crisis that served as a sign to become set apart. I can't say that I've audibly heard God speaking to me, or that, like John Wesley, I narrowly escaped a tragic accident. There were no early affirmations from others that I would make a fine pastor, counselor, or professor.

I can say that my heart has been strangely warmed, but often in unexpected places while I was doing ordinary things like sitting at the lake watching the sunset, having a conversation with a mother in a drug recovery program, listening to a homeless man's understanding of God as we drank coffee in the cold, or hearing the soulful notes of a street corner musician. One might wonder at this point what I've had besides moments of beauty, conversations with God, and traces of knowing which way to go or not go. "This doesn't sound like a call story," many might say. My answer is only this: I believe people can do many things in order to participate in Christian faith and the life of the church, but the deeper understanding of our call is the journey of a meaningful, shared life, and the call to be human.

This may seem almost backward, relating call to being instead of doing. And yet this is the only way I can talk about it. I hope that I am not misunderstood. I am not advocating a passive attitude toward life; rather, I am advocating for a more than surface-level or self-interested engagement in your own humanity and the humanity of others.

Call is movement. Call is understanding that what you do and where you do it may change, and yet God is still moving, speaking, listening, and working wherever you are.

Call is movement. Call is understanding that what you do and where you do it may change, and yet God is still moving, speaking, listening, and working wherever you are.

In today's world, there seem to be so many charismatic religious leaders, so much "show-and-tell" concerning material prosperity, so much focus on the megachurch phenomenon. And certainly the experience of such settings and events is dazzling, entertaining, exciting, even moving. Yet, I believe this is not the only way to be faithful and that to claim it is such is to have a narrow understanding of how call operates and is manifested. Jesus, after all, spent most of his life interacting with small, poor communities and shared his journey of life with only a few close friends and the occasional crowd of followers.

The affluence or "bling bling" of many U.S. lifestyles being justified by Bible verses reflects what I refer to as the glorified gospel

Women of Color Scholars

In 1987, the Black Clergywomen's Caucus of The United Methodist Church met in the Bahamas to bring to light some of the concerns involving black women and the church. One of the issues discussed was the lack of women of color faculty at United Methodist seminaries and theological schools. What began as a discussion resulted in a recommendation that the General Board of Higher Education and Ministry develop strategies to address this imbalance.

Through its Office of Loans and Scholarships and Division of Ordained Ministry, GBHEM created a scholarship program like none other— the Women of Color Scholars Program. Established to create a pool of trailblazing United Methodist women of color, many of whom are ordained clergy, more than twenty-two female scholars have successfully completed the program and set out on career paths in theological and religious education.

The program provides up to $10,000 a year in scholarship funds to selected women of color who are Ph.D. or Th.D. students. Any United Methodist woman having at least one parent of African, Hispanic, Native American, Asian or Pacific Islander background, who has earned a master of divinity degree and is pursuing a doctorate for a career in theological education and religious studies is eligible to apply.

To learn more, visit www.gbhem.org/woc.

of consumption. Consuming has become our way of life. We consume too much food, clothing, energy, information, television, Internet, products to make us look cool, cars, land, luxury items, and illusions of the good life. But the truth underneath the glorified gospel of consumption is that we don't need to consume as much as we do and we soon won't be able to consume as much as we have in the past. We have to get over having so many things; we need to stop hoarding the economic and natural resources of the world; we will have to relearn how to be.

Being human is going places with the attitude that there is always something you can learn from others. Being human is not acting as though you are the only person who has something valuable to offer. Being human is knowing that sometimes there are no words to undo a situation, but your willingness to cry or hold hands, laugh or sit in silence—your being there with all that you are is enough.

The call to be human is an invitation to participate in the New Creation. Wesley himself left room for such an understanding of call in his approach to sanctification. He considered sanctification to be not an event but rather a lifelong process that would lead us to a greater depth of spiritual growth and becoming more Christlike.

I don't want to overspiritualize what being in ministry actually is. There are times when you feel rejuvenated and free, while there are other times when you just feel frustrated, sleepy, and tired. There are times when your good intentions go wrong and times when you unknowingly have the most transformational impact on people's lives.

This is not a call story, not in the sense that there is a beginning, middle, and end. This is an invitation to be different, unfinished, open, curious, disappointed, surprised, outspoken, reflective, caring, funny, exhausted, sorrowful in solidarity with people who are not like you, forgiving, forgiven, helped by strangers, hopeful, changed. This is the journey of a meaningful, shared life with friends you encounter along the way. The call to be human is a process, not one without flaws or mistakes, but one where passion is expected, transformation is possible, and healing is necessary.

My hope for you as a young person discerning ministry in the church, the academy, or service in the world as your vocation is that you will be fully human in your reflection.

Elonda Clay is completing her Ph.D. in religion and science at the Lutheran School of Theology at Chicago. In addition to being a Fund for Theological Education doctoral fellow and United Methodist Women of Color Scholar, she is also a graduate of the Summer Leadership Institute at Harvard University. She has presented at international conferences as well as taught in local churches on religion and ecology, community technology, and genetics and identity. Her experiences of homelessness during childhood helped her to see the connections between poverty and the environment early in life and have informed her work within urban ministries and nonprofit organizations.

Hospital Ministry Has Taught Me About God's Grace

Ann G. Haywood-Baxter

After two years in the Peace Corps, I worked for one year as an elementary school media coordinator. I thought God was calling me to use my gifts as an elementary school educator and I was preparing to begin a master's degree in library science. But in my prayer life and in my worship experiences at the United Methodist church I was attending, I sensed that God was calling me to be more active in ministry.

I joined a small group and the teaching rotation for the adult Sunday school class that I attended. As a favor to one of my friends, I agreed to attend a women's retreat at the church. She needed a roommate for the retreat and she didn't want to be the only woman in her twenties attending.

To my great surprise, during the service of Holy Communion that was the closing worship of the retreat, I strongly sensed God calling me to ordained ministry. I was shocked and thought that people might laugh at me if I told them. When I returned home, I called several of my closest friends to see what they thought. To my amazement, everyone that I spoke with affirmed that they saw in me gifts for ordained ministry and encouraged me to further explore this calling.

After meeting with my pastor and my district superintendent, I formally began the exploration and candidacy process. Six months later, I began my theological studies at Duke Divinity School, assuming that I would serve as a pastor in a church following graduation.

During my first year in divinity school, my father was diagnosed with pancreatic cancer, undergoing major surgery in an attempt to save his life. I was with him and my mother during this intensely painful time—he experienced surgical complications during a three-week intensive care stay. Sadly, my father died and my heart was broken by this enormous loss. I was twenty-six years old and this was my first experience in an academic medical setting.

I had never before realized how complex a hospital stay could be. Because of my experience with my father, I knew I needed to study clinical pastoral care to better equip myself for when I would one day be a pastor visiting hospitalized church members.

In my third year of divinity school I worked at Duke University Hospital and loved it. My clinical pastoral care internship taught me a great deal. I learned from my supervisors, the patients, families, and the hospital caregivers. I discovered gifts for ministry in healthcare and discerned that I was being called to do a yearlong residency focusing on care at the end of life.

During my residency year I worked mostly with adult patients and their families in the medical intensive care unit. I decided to seek additional training, including a second residency focused on the care of pediatric patients and families. From the beginning of my time on the pediatric floors, I felt at home in my ministry and it was clear to me and to my supervisors that this was an area where I was called to serve in ministry.

With the support of my district superintendent, bishop, and board of ordained ministry, I was appointed to Massachusetts General Hospital where I serve as a chaplain to hospitalized children, their families, and their hospital caregivers. Each day I meet people from all over the world, from a variety of religious, cultural, and socioeconomic backgrounds, and I minister with people of all ages—premature babies, toddlers, school-age children, teens, and adults. Regardless of one's background or developmental stage, my ministry seeks to offer hospitality to strangers, connect people to their faith

> There are many, many patients, families, and hospital caregivers who have shaped my ministry and taught me about God's grace, God's faithfulness, and God's presence in the midst of suffering and uncertainty.

communities, and acknowledge God's presence even in the midst of a busy academic medical setting.

There are many, many patients, families, and hospital caregivers who have shaped my ministry and taught me about God's grace, God's faithfulness, and God's presence in the midst of suffering and uncertainty. I remember a young girl, who I will call Shante, asking me, "Are you an angel?" I was surprised by her question and answered, "No, I'm not an angel. I'm a chaplain—a minister who works in the hospital. I am a friend to kids and their families; my job is to remind people that God loves them very much." Two days earlier, Shante had been hit by a car on her way to school. Her right leg had to be amputated.

Ann G. Haywood-Baxter confers with a hospital staff member.

During our first meeting Shante asked me to pray for her. She told me she was having trouble sleeping because she was scared. I held her hand, listened to her fears, and prayed with her. I told her that sometimes people select a phrase to say to themselves over and over again whenever they feel scared. Some people choose sentences like "The Lord is my Shepherd" or "God is with me." Shante liked this idea and she decided that her breath prayer would be "Angels surround me."

When I visited again the following day Shante greeted me with the same question. "Are you an angel?" As I reminded her of my role as a hospital chaplain, she held my hand and smiled. "I think you are an angel. Angels surround me."

The following Sunday, I shared this story with my pastor. He reminded me that the Greek word for *angel* means "messenger" and he suggested that Shante might be right. As a chaplain, my message, shared through pastoral presence, song, worship, education, play, listening, and sacramental ministry, is "You are loved" and "You are not alone." I am grateful for the opportunity to serve as a messenger of Christ's love and abiding presence, and I am grateful for the lessons of faith that I continue to learn from those whom I serve.

Ann G. Haywood-Baxter is an elder in the Western North Carolina Conference of The United Methodist Church and pediatric chaplain at Massachusetts General Hospital in Boston. She is a graduate of Duke Divinity School and Wake Forest University, completed her Clinical Pastoral Education at Duke University Medical Center, and is a board certified chaplain. Ann and her husband, Richard Baxter, are active in the ministries of Harvard-Epworth United Methodist Church in Cambridge, Mass.

Who Are Chaplains and Pastoral Counselors?

Chaplains and pastoral counselors are elders or deacons who engage in ministries of pastoral care in specialized settings.

Where Do They Serve?

Endorsed chaplains and pastoral counselors are appointed to prisons, hospitals, the armed forces, and counseling centers where they serve people in difficult places outside the local church.

What Do Chaplains and Pastoral Counselors Do?

In more than sixteen different civilian settings and in all areas of the military, chaplains and pastoral counselors care for those who are hurting physically, mentally, emotionally, and spiritually.

Below are some of the endorsed settings where they serve:

- Health-care chaplains are spiritual companions with patients and their families. They listen and discern how the spirit of God may be working in patients' lives. They administer sacraments upon request and provide opportunities for worship, spiritual reflection, and celebration. They work with doctors, nurses, psychiatrists, and social workers to advocate for the patient. They work to help all the hospital staff understand pastoral care and the spiritual dimensions of illness, suffering, and death.

- Military chaplains live out Wesley's words "The world is my parish" in real and personal ways. Their ministry is incarnational in that they live, sleep, eat, sail, and march with their congregation. They work alongside people from many faith groups in diverse settings that give an opportunity to observe God's work through people with different outlooks. Military chaplains go to all corners of the world to deliver rites, sacraments, and services to all who are in need and would otherwise be far from a local church.

- Correctional chaplains serve in unique and diverse communities to preach, teach, baptize, serve Communion, counsel, visit, and serve the prison congregation. They minister to inmates, staff, and families, and are the link between religious communities outside and inside prisons, jails, or detention facilities.

- Pastoral counselors are trained in theology and as professional mental-health counselors. They serve in counseling centers, on the staff of local churches, and in health-care institutions working with individuals, families, and groups where their counseling is within the tradition, beliefs, and resources of the faith community. Their ministry includes counseling and interpretation, biblical storytelling, speaking truth to the powerful, listening attentively to the sacred stories presented by those in the counseling space, and responding as God's representative.

How Do They Find Work?

Generally, chaplains and pastoral counselors are required to be ordained, to complete specialized training for a specific setting, and to receive the church's endorsement through the United Methodist Endorsing Agency (UMEA), General Board of Higher Education and Ministry. Endorsement is both a process and a relationship that determines readiness for pastoral ministry in specialized settings.

As with all ordained persons, chaplains and pastoral counselors are appointed to serve by the bishop of the annual conference through which they are ordained.

I Was *Compelled* Into Ministry

Matt Miofsky

I t is 1 a.m. and I am in my office. I am a pastor and I feel a strange obligation to stay at the church until everyone else is gone. I take off my vestments, sit in my chair, and, almost as a reflex, roll up to my computer to check my e-mail. The inbox is empty. It is Christmas Day, and normal people are sleeping. I laugh to myself. I sit there a bit longer and stare at my bookshelf, thinking about the classes that each book represents. I remember a seminary professor who once said that a theologian can never guard against every possible misunderstanding. I took that to mean that you cannot say everything that needs to be said at one time. I have always liked that. I look up at the two degrees from high-priced universities hanging in mahogany frames on my wall. I laugh again.

I walk out of my office realizing that the 200 or so people gathered for our third and last Christmas Eve worship service are now gone. The church is empty and I can go home. So I begin to walk. It is cold, much more so than a typical Christmas. I pull down my stocking cap and bury my face in my coat and walk. It is not much of a walk, though. My house is right next door. I laugh for a third time—a kind of holy laughter, like Sarah's, the laugh of one mystified by the absurdity of God's plans for her. On this night it's the absurdity of my life that hits me as I walk. It all seems ironic . . . or is *bizarre* a better word? Did I mention that it is one in the morning? How did I end up here?

Curiosity is a funny but apt word to describe my motivation for entering the ministry. Religion was never forced on me, nor was my family extreme in their piety. Midwest pragmatism did not allow for that. Nonetheless, church, and my participation in it, was never optional. My mother and father taught Sunday school, served on committees, cooked for church dinners and cleaned up when they were done. The by-product of such volunteerism was that my brother and I loitered around the church more than most. Like a child who grows up in a bilingual household, you tend to learn the different languages, regardless of whether or not you want to.

There are too many childhood stories about church to recall, and like home movies, they are not always as exciting to hear as they are to share. But it is enough to say that I was raised in the church and when you are raised in the church *choice* is not a useful word. I cannot recall choosing to be in the church. I don't remember choosing to use the language I learned there to interpret my life and life's work. I don't remember choosing to be moved by the music, compelled by the Scriptures, or formed by the sense of community. I don't remember choosing it to be an integral part of the very fiber of my being.

Looking back, I see the way this drama of my call was being written, oftentimes by forces not completely within my control, and the force of my environment and the way it shaped and molded me, predisposing me to feel, think, and act in particular ways. I see the force of my own choices, the times when, standing at a crossroads,

I made decisions, or perhaps it's better to say that decisions were squeezed out of me. I see the force of the Holy Spirit luring my curiosity and passion with beauty, delight, justice, pain, and the possibility of redemption.

If I had to pick a verb that describes my entrance into ministry, a verb that explains how I moved from a small town in Missouri that valued hard work, American notions of success, and football, to a university replete with endless opportunities and plenty of bright people ready to seize them, to a graduate school that flooded my head with ideas, to a church office at one o'clock in the morning, the verb is *compelled*.

I was *compelled* to go into the ministry.

My college experience was ironically formative for me. Ironic in that the university I attended was an aggressively secular institution. Formative because it was in this atmosphere I most acutely experienced being the church. Like many, the academic study of religion intrigued me with questions my Sunday school teachers had never asked, much less answered. There was only one man on our campus who consistently taught courses on Christianity. But as I studied religion, I felt the haunting indictment that my curiosity-driven interest was decidedly anemic if it did not also include some commitment. I could not merely be curious about God; faith demands more than even an active curiosity.

And so this one professor would leave a peculiar mark on me, not in his role as my teacher, mentor, or even friend. It was something quite unexpected that changed me. One day, I walked to our campus chapel for a rare college-sponsored worship opportunity. Several clergy sat stoically around an austere altar in various vestments appropriate to their traditions. But none of them rose when it came time to read the gospel. Instead, dressed in his hallmark earthy-colored sport coat (yes, the kind with patches on the elbow) my professor stood to read the gospel. When finished, he closed the Bible and did something that I will never forget. He preached.

I have no idea what he preached about; I cannot remember what he said. But that was unimportant. It was not memorable because of what he preached, but rather *that* he preached. It was the first time my suspicions about the nature of his commitment were confirmed. He was not only a brilliant and curious scholar, he had a commitment to the content of what he taught. He believed in the church, and, in a strange way, seeing his belief gave me motivation and permission to also believe. He was crucial in turning my curiosity into commitment—a commitment that played out in surprising ways.

When it came down to "deciding," I knew that as much as I wanted to make a lot of money, have autonomy over where I worked and lived, provide easily for my future family, feasibly pay off my student loans, work in a field that would be instantly respected by those around me, and be home in bed at a reasonable hour on Christmas Eve, I could not resist the compelling nature of ministry. What finally drew me to the vocation of ministry was the disparity between its claims and the ones implied by a medley of other disciplines and fields. At a university that heavily valued science and reason, the claims made by a seemingly isolated group of religious thinkers seemed impractical. The context only accentuated the distinctness, even foolishness, of God's claims about the world, and I wanted my life to embody that distinction. Could my life become a witness for something different? Maybe a different way of living, or perhaps just a different way of seeing and valuing the world.

It is one in the morning again, now almost three weeks after Christmas. I skate across the icy parking lot from my house to the church where eighty kids are hanging out at a lock-in. I talked with some kids and played basketball with a few others. As I was leaving, the teenagers were gathering to worship. As the music began, some kids were giggling, others reluctantly tore themselves away from the snack bar, and one just lay down as if to nap, rolling his eyes and settling into a comfortable position. A few of the kids stood up and sang, eyes closed, hands clutched together, and I knew they were looking for something. I listened for a moment and inconspicuously slipped out the back door and began my walk.

It's cold tonight, bright from the moon, but cold. I wonder about God's sense of humor sometimes, placing my home right next to the church, giving me the gifts, intellectual and otherwise, to do anything I choose, only to leave me without a choice. It is ironic I guess, or maybe *bizarre* is a better word, comical in a holy way. Whatever it is, it is home for now. There are many other places I could be, perhaps even that I might rather be. But none of them is as compelling as this place. I am certain of it; God has a sense of humor. Did I mention it is one in the morning? What am I doing here? I sit back in my chair . . . and laugh.

Matt Miofsky is pastor of The Gathering, a new United Methodist church in St. Louis, Missouri. You can visit it online at gatheringnow.org. Matt and his wife, Jessica, have three children, Caleb, Carly, and George.

No Lightbulbs, Just a Lifetime Awareness of God's Call

Sarah McQueen

There are no lightbulbs in the story of my call. Others can name a physical place where they were sitting when God called them to ministry. Instead of a single flash of insight, I have been aware throughout my entire life that God is shaping and forming me for servant ministry.

My faith journey began early. I was baptized as an infant in both the Roman Catholic and United Methodist traditions. My maternal grandparents advocated that I be trained in the Roman Catholic faith, but due to scheduling I usually attended my father's United Methodist church. My parents supported my exploration of faith by encouraging me to participate fully in The United Methodist Church, but also in programs at Baptist, Free Evangelical, and Episcopal churches. Being active in so many different churches allowed me to explore what was the same and what was different among denominations. I developed an academic interest in church in addition to my spiritual interest.

During the eighth-grade Sunday school class at Cherrydale United Methodist Church, in Arlington, Virginia, our teacher attempted to help us meet God, greet God, and lean on God. Learning about the spiritual walks of my peers helped me realize that because each person is created differently we experience God in a variety of ways. My passion is to help people from young to old discover how they experience God's presence in their lives.

My passion is to help people from young to old
discover how they experience God's presence in their lives.

Initially, I thought my passion for spiritual formation meant that I should serve as a director of Christian education, and my studies in college were completed with that goal in mind. During my study abroad experience at Oxford University I heard the distinct call to incorporate mission work into my ministry. Just when I could envision my future life in response to God's call to full-time Christian service, I attended Virginia's EXPLORATION 2002, an event for young people considering a call to ordained ministry. That experience stirred up a calling toward ordination. I also realized that my calling isn't a static message that just needs clarification, but rather a continual conversation with God regarding life's journey.

I entered the candidacy process in order for discernment as an ordained deacon in Christian education or in music. For one year I served as a ministry intern at Annandale United Methodist Church. Working there allowed me to explore the professional areas of the church, specifically the areas of music and education. In tandem with prayer and mentoring, that internship opened my heart to the calling of ordination as an elder.

My passions for music and spiritual formation are indeed assets to the role of an elder in The United Methodist Church, but they are not the foundations of my call to ordination. Living a life of interpretation is what I feel God has placed on my heart. The responsibility of engaging Scripture for interpretation to a community, living in relationship with others as a companion for the faith journey, being involved with mission work, and working for social justice are all part of my life of interpretation. Looking for God's presence in everyday life and exploring this presence in the lives of other people are important to my call as an elder. Administering the sacraments and exploring God's mysterious presence as a reality in our world are important to my sense of call to ministry.

Last year, during my field education supervisor's vacation, I had the opportunity to take primary responsibility for leading worship and pastoring the church. One Sunday morning during this time I felt peace wash over—a sense that I was exactly where God called me to be, and that I had a lifetime of opportunity to continue living out that calling. I look forward to helping guide a congregation into living out their call to be a part of God's kingdom. Serving as a parish minister means that I will be able to engage with a community in living a deeper and richer life that bears the reality of God's presence in our life and in our world.

Sarah McQueen graduated from Boston University's School of Theology and is a provisional elder in the Virginia Annual Conference. She loves all things Mac, Club Bridge, and Taizé.

Mentor Saw Potential in Me That I Didn't See

Matthew L. Kelley

You're not going to any church right now? Cool! You're our newest member!"

I had known Will Penner for all of ten minutes and he was already recruiting me to be part of his youth group. I didn't protest. After spending ten minutes with this youth group and their youth director, I knew there was something there I wanted to be a part of. Those ten minutes helped set the course for the next ten years of my life.

It was true. I hadn't been going to any church for a while. Near the end of my junior year in high school, and for a variety of reasons, I had drifted away from the church in which I had grown up. Though the reasons for this were many, it basically came down to the fact that I didn't feel at home there anymore. For a couple months I floated around not really knowing what to do. Sundays were especially depressing, because church had been such a big part of my life ever since I had dedicated my life to serving God on a mission trip at age thirteen.

I wasn't sure where God was leading me next, only that it was somewhere different from what I'd known before. So when a friend invited me to her church's party after our school's football game, I decided to go for the heck of it, and within ten minutes I discovered that this was where God wanted me to be.

After a few weeks as part of this new youth group, Will surprised me again. I was hanging out with him after youth group one Sunday evening, practicing some new worship songs on the guitar when he started asking me what I planned on doing with my future. I said I wasn't really sure, so Will decided that since I was a senior, I would become his assistant and learn how to be a youth pastor.

For the rest of my senior year, I watched and learned as Will explained how he planned weekly youth meetings, led Bible studies, visited school campuses, and interacted with the senior pastor and other staff. I even filled in for him in his other role as choir director when he was absent one Sunday, despite having zero experience at conducting. I figured that this experience would help prepare me for a possible church job later on in life. What I didn't know was that "later on" would be a few months down the road.

The summer after graduation I was working at a church camp when a church group from Indianapolis, where I would begin college in the fall, ended the camp week by offering me a job. I had grown close to the youth and adults from this church during the week, and since they were looking for a new youth director, they decided to offer me the job even though neither their pastor nor a single member of their Staff-Parish Relations Committee was in camp that week. The fact that I was eighteen years old, straight out of high school, barely older than some of the kids, and had zero experience didn't seem to matter (although my innumerable rookie mistakes may have made them question their choice later on).

Matthew L. Kelley visits the South Street Seaport Museum while on vacation in New York.

The first thing I did as soon as I got home was to make a frantic phone call to Will. "What do I do?" I asked, freaking out about taking on an actual "adult" role. Will couldn't comprehend why I was so worried. "You've spent the past year watching what I do and practicing it yourself. You know what to do."

Will was right, at least in part. I knew how to run a decent youth group meeting. I could plan and lead a Bible study. I could rehearse a praise band and organize mission trips and fund-raisers. But at the same time, I didn't know how to "be" a pastor to youth and their families. I didn't know what to do when I got a frantic phone call or e-mail from a teenager in crisis. I knew how to do the nuts and bolts of ministry, but the more intangible aspects were a mystery to me.

Thankfully, Will was there for me then, too. During my first year in youth ministry I probably called him at least once a week grilling him with questions on everything from how to deal with an agitated parent to how to delicately address youth being dressed inappropriately for church. What I began to learn is that while you can learn the basic functions of ministry by watching someone else do them and practicing a bit, the more intangible parts, the "being" of ministry, if you will, is a lot more complicated. You don't learn how to handle most situations until you're in them, so you figure it

I didn't know what to do when I got a frantic phone call or e-mail from a teenager in crisis. I knew how to do the nuts and bolts of ministry, but the more intangible aspects were a mystery to me.

out as you go. If you handle them well, you figure out why and make sure to repeat those actions in the future. If you mess up (which you will more often than not), you process, regroup, learn from your mistakes, apologize if need be, and do better the next time.

I could have learned all about the "doing" of ministry from a book or a training seminar. There is no shortage of good ones out there. The "doing" is relatively easy. But I never could have learned about the "being" of ministry without a mentor who was willing to take me under his wing, allowing me to watch and learn from what he did, and having the patience and grace to endure my endless questioning and self-doubt once I was out on my own. This mentoring relationship has given me valuable insights that the best book or class never could.

In the ten years since I walked into that youth group party, my life has changed dramatically. I have graduated from college and seminary.

My own understanding of calling has led me to go from being a youth pastor, to an associate pastor, and eventually to being pastor of my own congregation. Will is still active in youth ministry, and I still talk with him often and seek his advice. I've met and learned from other mentors along the way. But none of this would have happened had I not met a mentor who helped me begin discerning my calling by seeing potential in me that I didn't see in myself.

Matthew L. Kelley is pastor of Bethlehem United Methodist Church in Clarksville, Tennessee. He has a B.A. in religion and political science from Butler University and an M.Div. from Vanderbilt University.

God Calls Us Through the Familiar and the Strange

Renita Thomas

t was the last night of a spirited, weeklong fall revival in a small town in Georgia. The revival features lively harmonious singing and a popular revivalist, the Rev. Cornelius Henderson, who brings rhythmic preaching, infectious energy, and magnetic charisma. (Before his death years later, Henderson became a bishop in The United Methodist Church.)

An exuberant congregation closes out this Friday night worship in grand fashion. All the lights in the church have been turned off, the doors are locked, and it's all over.

Another revival comes to an end. But I'm still there. Why?

I don't know. I'm standing on the landing of the outside entrance of Wesley Chapel United Methodist Church. A twenty-one-year-old college graduate of only seven days, I stand with a stranger and one of my childhood girlfriends. She introduces me to the

Candidacy for Ordained Ministry In The United Methodist Church

Each person feels God's call in a different way. However the invitation comes, you have to decide how you will answer. Is God calling you to use your gifts and talents as a deacon or elder?

You also need honest feedback. Talk with your family, friends, and your pastor, or another clergyperson. Share your thoughts with these people and ask their advice.

Once you are ready to take the next step, you will start the candidacy process—the first formal step toward ordination (as a deacon or an elder) or licensing in The United Methodist Church.

Contact your pastor, another elder or deacon, or the superintendent of the district in which your United Methodist church, campus ministry, or faith community is located to inquire about the candidacy process. Visit www.gbhem.org/beginning candidacy for a detailed description of the process.

stranger and he and I begin to talk. With his prompting, I find myself telling him all about my experience with church and my involvement in college with the United Methodist Wesley Foundation Campus Ministry. I also tell him of my plans to start looking for a job on Monday morning in the field of social work. He mentions that he is the president and dean of Gammon Theological Seminary, a United Methodist seminary in Atlanta. I find out that he has been at the revival all week. I wonder, "Why haven't we met earlier in the week?"

We continue to talk. During our conversation, he suggests that I should consider getting a dual master's degree in divinity and sociology. Meanwhile, my internal dialogue was, "Have I ever heard of seminary? Have I even considered graduate school? What?"

Then I think to myself, "He's crazy, I just finished

college a week ago; no way am I going back to school that soon."
We continue to talk. He gives me a card and invites me to visit him at
Gammon on Monday. As we depart I think to myself, "What a strange
conversation!" When I get home I share with my parents this strange,
crazy encounter. They question me as if I'm the strange, crazy one.
Even though I haven't decided if I am going to make this visit, they
both ask, "Do you know what you are doing?" I think to myself,
"Not really."

Somehow God is using this stranger to take me
down a path I never knew existed for me. It was God's yes,
to my great questioning.

Where is this coming from? Did God send this stranger? I
wrestle with God all weekend long—praying, thinking, and toiling,
and praying, thinking, and toiling some more, trying to discern
whether I will go and talk with this stranger on Monday. I finally say
to God late Sunday night, "God, I'm going to talk to this man on
Monday, and then you can't say that I didn't try." I drive to Atlanta
on Monday and meet with this stranger.

By Monday afternoon I am enrolled in seminary. No transcript,
no money, no housing. It was just me and the Good Lord nudging
me through this stranger's invitation. Somehow God is using this
stranger to take me down a path I never knew existed for me. It was
God's yes, to my great questioning.

I go back home and announce the news to my parents. With
great concern, they question me once more, "Do you know what

you are doing?" Secretly questioning myself I say, "God knows."

Without taking time to hesitate or think, I start seminary the next day—this young woman who believed that on Monday she was headed for a job in social work. I commute from home my first year. My pastor is supportive and encourages me to make sure I follow the process into ordained ministry. He gives me opportunities to preach and do projects for my seminary work. He even insists that the church pay me as a student pastor. By my second year I get a denominational academic scholarship that covers tuition, and room and board. I do work study for other expenses.

I experience seminary as intriguing, challenging, informative, and transformative. I later recognize I wouldn't have exchanged that time for anything in the world. Thank God for divine intrusion into my life journey.

Now here's the background to my story. I grew up in The Methodist Episcopal Church, South, and then The United Methodist Church from the time I was two years old. My mother taught Sunday school and she made sure my brother and I were there every Sunday. My father served on various committees in the church, and my godmother was the church secretary, so I spent many Saturdays folding church bulletins. I accepted Jesus as my savior and officially joined the church when I was ten. I walked right down the aisle on my own and a few weeks later I was baptized. I participated in church plays, Sunday school, Bible study, vacation Bible school, and the youth and young adult choir, among other church activities. At home, when I wasn't busy with chores or homework, I would lie across the bed and take the Methodist hymnal and sing all the hymns that I knew. When I was old enough, I sat near the back of the church with my friends during worship and giggled and made fun of the senior choir and talked about things that had nothing to do with worship. Eventually, I went off to college and by my sophomore year had declared on one of my weekend trips back home in the combined Sunday school class of adults and young adults that "I didn't know about this God. I wasn't sure that God existed but I was going to check it out." The adults didn't pounce on me with a "Young lady, that's not the way we think around here." They just listened and continued to love me.

No one ever told me I was going to be a preacher when I grew up and I hadn't been exposed to any female preachers in The United Methodist Church. I was clueless that God would call me to serve in the church. I had no idea I would be going to seminary and no idea that one day I would be leading others to Jesus through serving the church as an ordained minister. Yet four church appointments later—an associate pastor position, a pastor position, and two annual conference positions, totaling twenty-four years—and after many other ministry experiences, here I am writing this account of my call story. I see my call as a gradual preparation through having grown up in a loving church family and this all-of-a-sudden moment of God's redirecting my journey, led by a stranger, Dr. Major Jones, who I came to know as a friend and mentor. God's call comes in many and varied ways. God calls us through the familiar and the strange, through calm and chaos. God will call you. And God is able to do exceedingly, abundantly more than we could ever ask for or imagine.

Renita Thomas is currently serving as an associate director in the North Georgia Conference Office of Connectional Ministries. She loves life and values much the opportunity to be in ministry with all of God's people.

I Felt a Tug in My Being at Foot-washing Service

Sara Baron

It started when I was thirteen, at our United Methodist church camp, Sky Lake. The camp was a familiar place, but I was in a music camp I hadn't come to before, and in a group where I didn't know anyone else. I was feeling shy, and there were too many campers in the group for the counselors to really notice me. It was the first night of camp and everyone was gathered at the waterfront for a foot-washing service, something I'd never experienced before.

I sat looking at the lake, sitting next to the oar-house, with my arm resting on an old, black inner tube, and listening as the camp director spoke. She talked about Jesus as a different kind of leader, saying that most leaders expect people to serve them, but Jesus turned that upside down when he served others. She started to talk about servant leadership, in which a follower of Christ doesn't lead with power, but with gentleness and love. Then, one by one, the director and my counselor for that week washed all the feet of the campers and staff.

We were singing softly as they washed those feet. It was during the song "Sanctuary," also new to me at the time, that I began an internal conversation, speaking to and answering myself.

"This foot-washing service is so powerful, I wish I could be a part of it."

Somehow God is using this stranger to take me

down a path I never knew existed for me. It was God's yes,

to my great questioning.

"It is powerful, but look at the women leading it. You have to be a pastor to wash feet." (Clearly I didn't understand the role of a pastor yet.)

"That's true. Oh well, I still wish I could be part of it."

"Well, maybe I could. If I were a pastor."

"I can't be a pastor! I have all these things I want to do. I want to be a scientist like my mother. I want to own a house. I want to be able to make my own decisions. I can't be a pastor."

"I can't. . . . Well, I could."

"But what about the Ph.D.? And the house? And the freedom?"

"I don't know."

Truthfully, I don't remember having my feet washed, or anything much about the rest of that week of camp. The next part of my call came eleven months later, at Wyoming Annual Conference. Our camp had been invited to sing at the ordination service. (Incidentally, I can't sing. When I went to camp, I didn't know I'd have to

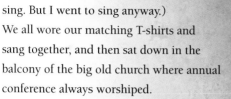

sing. But I went to sing anyway.)
We all wore our matching T-shirts and
sang together, and then sat down in the
balcony of the big old church where annual
conference always worshiped.

At the end of the service the bishop offered
an altar call to those who were considering
ordained ministry. I felt a tug in my being. I had
almost forgotten that talk with myself on the beach,
but with the same group of people, it came back with
stunning clarity. I was drawn to the altar, to respond,
to admit what I was feeling. But I wasn't ready. Those
other things were still holding me back—the desire
to be a scientist, the desire for a house of my own,
and my freedom. So I told God that I wasn't going to
respond to the call—this year! But, I promised to
think about it all year long, and show up back at the
same service the following year to give my answer.

I told my brother about my experience a few
days later, sitting in the car in the parking lot of
the grocery store while our parents shopped
after church. He laughed at me, telling me that
it was the stupidest thing he'd ever heard, and
that I should do something useful with my
life instead. I kept my mouth shut after that,
but I did manage to tell my pastor that I
wanted to go to annual conference, and he
got me set up as a youth delegate.

Again, the story took a pause,
until the following year at the
annual conference ordination
service. I was at the
service with the

rest of the youth, sitting next to my best friend, who still makes fun of me for this. The altar call had begun, and we were both crying with the magnetic pull we felt to the altar and the strength of the feeling. We let our hair hang down so that no one else would see the tears, although really we were so busy trying to hide our own tears that we didn't notice that others were crying too. There were several songs picked out to sing during the altar call, and the last one was completed. I hadn't managed to move yet, so I said to God, "Oh well, too late, maybe next year."

The bishop responded, "It's not too late." I pushed my best friend out of the way in my rush to get to the altar. Once I was there, I was sure. There was to be no turning back for me. The things I did afterward, like Chrysalis and Disciple, just affirmed my decision. My parents, unlike my brother, were fully supportive.

As I think about it though, the call itself didn't come full circle until five years later, seven years after I started hearing it. I was back at camp, back on the beach, back with the same director. We hadn't done a foot-washing service in all those intervening years, but we were doing one again. I'd grown up. Instead of being a shy, first-time music camper, I was a senior member with many years' experience. I was going into my last year of college, with seminary on the horizon.

There were more campers than we used to have, and so there were four foot-washing stations and the entire staff was split up to make the process smooth and efficient. I was assigned to walk campers from the bench where they removed their shoes to the director's station. After a while, she motioned for me to stay with the camper. After he left, she whispered to me that she needed to get up (she wasn't well that summer) and I needed to kneel in the lake, and wash feet so that she could rest.

My dream had come full circle. The initial urge toward ordained ministry came in my confusion about the sacramental nature of washing feet. As I knelt and washed the feet of campers, I felt God moving through me to offer humble blessing. It was astonishing to feel that power. Yet I realized as I did it that the call may have started as a desire to wash feet, but over the years, it had become a desire to serve as an elder of the church. The call had grown with me, and although the original desire was fulfilled, it had just been a step on the way.

Sara Baron is a provisional elder serving a small church in upstate New York. She directs the camp where she once heard the call and makes sure to have a foot washing as part of Holy Week worship.

When the Phone Rang, It Was God's Call

Margaret Davis Freeman

I didn't know it then, but when the phone rang, it was a call from God.

It was spring of my senior year in college, and I was feeling pretty down. All my friends had decided what they would be doing after graduation, and had great plans. Some had good-paying jobs already lined up, one was going on to law school, another to medical school, and they had things all figured out. Not me!

I had gone home over a school break, and spent lots of time talking with my mother about what I might do. I remember her saying to me, "Don't worry. God will lead you in the direction you are to go. You just have to be open to listen." I wasn't really sure what she meant, but my reply was something like, "I'm ready for God to lead me, but I just wish God would call me on the phone or something!"

Several days later, back at school, I was immersed once again in the midst of all my friends' plans after graduation. They were talking about where they would be living, what they would be doing, and how great life was.

I had to get away from all of that, and the only place I could be alone was in the shower. That was the longest shower I have ever taken, as I cried tears of frustration, hopelessness, and inadequacy. What was wrong with me that I couldn't figure out what I wanted to do with my life? I had started off with a major in psychology, knowing that I was interested in people, and that I wanted to do something to help others. After taking a religion course my junior year, I decided to add religion to my major as I really enjoyed talking and thinking about God, and wanted to take more courses in the religion department. But now as the end of college was near, I wasn't sure that majoring in psychology and religion was going to get me very far.

While I was crying my heart out and feeling sorry for myself in the shower, my roommate knocked on the door. I didn't want to let on that I had been crying, so I wrapped one towel around my body and another loosely over my head and face as I opened the door. She held the phone in her hand and indicated some man was on the phone. As I answered the phone, dripping water all over the floor, I heard the familiar voice of my pastor from home.

My first thought was that something had happened, because why would he be calling me while I was away at college? After a few pleasantries, he asked me if I would prayerfully consider something. Of course I would—wasn't my pastor asking me to? He went on to say that an endowment fund had been created with the specific purpose of funding a one-year internship in youth ministry, and that the Pastor-Parish Relations Committee and my youth minister had identified me as the person they would like to take the position.

Furthermore, he stated, "I believe you have the gifts and graces for ministry." I had no idea what he was talking about, and I very flippantly replied, "I have never been called graceful, but I'm always ready to receive gifts!"

At that point, I had never seen a female pastor, and had no concept of what that might look like, or how that fit me. Not wanting to be rude, I asked him if I could think more about the internship, talk with my parents, and pray about it for a couple of days. Sensing that he had caught me completely off guard, he suggested that I might want to talk with my youth minister, which I did as soon as I hung up the phone.

After much prayer, conversation with family and friends, and long walks, I decided that I would accept the position. What did I have to lose? I could live with my parents for a year, save up money, and then move to some other place with an exciting job, just as my friends were doing.

I didn't realize it at the time, but that phone call was God calling me into ministry. I spent that year working in my home church, where I grew in ways I never knew possible. I was excited about going to work every day, and discovered new skills. Besides, I was surrounded by a variety of people, was doing something to help others, *and* was using my major in psychology and religion.

At the end of that year, the church offered me a permanent full-time position, but I felt I needed more education. I still had not seen a female pastor, and wasn't sure exactly what the future held, but I knew I wanted to make a commitment before God and my church family at the altar of my church. I wanted to commit to a lifetime of full-time service to God. As I stood at that altar, with my pastor offering a blessing for me, I knew that God was calling, and I was ready to respond.

As I continued my education, pursuing a master's degree in Christian education, I began to explore the possibility of diaconal ministry. That seemed perfect for me, as I saw myself wanting to serve in the midst of God's people, helping them to discover their gifts and use them for ministry as members of the body of Christ. After completing graduate school, I was consecrated a diaconal minister.

Margaret Davis Freeman teaches a confirmation class.

For many years, serving as a diaconal minister seemed a perfect fit. I was serving in the midst of the laity and connecting them to serve both in the church and out in the world. However, I began having a nagging feeling that there was more that God wanted me to do. I knew I wasn't called to preach every Sunday and to order a church, but there was still something missing as I served in ministry.

When the separate orders of deacon and elder were created at General Conference in 1996, I paid close attention. The office of deacon seemed to have been created for me, as I saw my gifts of teaching, serving, and helping connect others to ministry. After much prayer and conversation with others, while at a discernment event, once again I was crying and asking God to tell me what I should do. It was in the midst of those tears and reading Scripture that I felt a real sense of peace come over me, and I knew that I was to say yes to ordination as a full-connection deacon.

I have been amazed at how God has worked through me. Whether serving on staff in a local church, doing consulting work, or leading retreats and workshops, I feel like God has provided a way for me to use my gifts in a variety of ways.

I have grown in my faith, been energized by those times when working with others as the body of Christ, and been blessed beyond measure by seeing persons experience a connection with Christ and use their gifts for ministry, both as laity and clergy. How thankful I am that I *did* take that phone call so many years ago, and stepped aside to allow God to work in me and through me. I am so glad that the line wasn't busy, or that I didn't say I would return the call later!

I now know that God calls us in a variety of ways and through different voices—we just need to be open to hear and ready to respond.

Margaret Davis Freeman has a passion for helping others respond to God's call and to do their best in ministry. She is a clergy member in the North Georgia Annual Conference of The United Methodist Church. Over the past twenty-seven years, she has served in churches in Georgia, Arkansas, Texas, and Tennessee and is currently appointed to First United Methodist Church in Franklin, North Carolina, as minister of discipleship.

God Fueled the Fire of Call on My Life

Michelle Bodle

Since my early childhood, I have looked ahead and had a plan for the future. I distinctly remember being three years old, having my dad lie on the couch with a place mat on his forehead and a play stethoscope around my neck. From that moment I knew I was supposed to be a doctor. My dream changed slightly over the years, as I declared my specialty to be psychiatry in tenth grade, but through the years I fervently pursued being a doctor, going as far as to attend an elite summer program between my junior and senior years of high school for future medical professionals. I was so engulfed in my vision that I ignored all inklings of a calling to ministry in my life.

I had other personal reasons for ignoring the call. My parents have always been active in the local church. My dad served as lay speaker and Sunday school teacher and my mother co-led youth group. Around fifth grade our local church started to put immense pressure on my brothers and me to step up to the example that my parents had set in service and leadership. I started to be placed in leadership roles that nowadays no longer would be allowed, including teaching fifth graders in an afterschool program when I was in only sixth grade.

By my senior year of high school, I was burned out from ministry and the expectations of my church family. I was no longer being spiritually nurtured so I started attending another church just so I could have enough energy to continue in a minimized number of ministries. In this church I found that my heart was being tugged toward areas of compassion and social justice work.

These desires to work for social justice intensified as I attended college in a city in great need of mercy and compassion. My heart broke for people as I walked down the streets, so during my freshman year in college I became a social advocate. I began to search the Bible for words concerning the poor and tried to put them into action. I also yearned to see the church become passionate about serving the poor and stopping social injustices around the world.

That first year of college, I had the unique opportunity to live immersed in the hurting city of Pittsburgh and experience a church whose hearts broke for those they ministered to at the Open Door. I began to spend all of my free time working for the church and the local children's hospital. Around October of my freshman year I became keenly aware that I was being called to work for the church. My desire to go into medicine diminished and a new vision emerged of being a lay minister. Due to some uneasy feelings I still had from watching my parents serve in the church, I continued to push aside the call to full-time ministry. I thought I could serve as a lay minister and still hold a primary job as a psychologist. However, I did not want to be trained to be a psychologist by the university I was attending, so I transferred to Houghton College—a private, Christian, liberal arts college in New York—as a double major in psychology and religion.

As I tried to discern my call I attended the God's Call conference event at the urging of my pastor. The first time I attended the event, I left feeling irritated because so much emphasis was placed on being a church pastor. If anything, at that point in time I felt that I was being called to be a lay speaker or lay minister, but I did leave the event with much-needed peace about transferring colleges.

Up until the end of my first semester of my junior year of college I still intended to serve as a lay minister. However, as I started to look at graduate schools in psychology around Thanksgiving time I came to the realization that God had been aligning my life to be a pastor and not a psychologist. He was going to use my psychological training in a unique way in the setting of the church. After much prayer and consultation with those closest to me, I found that they also had a sense that I should not pursue psychology as a primary field of work any longer. As that door shut, I started my candidacy process to be a pastor.

Even as I have worked through my candidacy process the past couple of months, I have seen God's plan for my life develop into something completely different from what I could have ever imagined. Doors have been opening up to work with missions organizations that emphasize social justice and community. I have felt called to seminaries I never thought I would attend. And I have felt a pull in my heart to serve as a pastor for an indefinite period of time before returning to school to obtain a doctorate in theology and eventually teach theology at the college or seminary level.

Through all of this I have learned that God's plans are more exciting and complete than anything I could ever have imagined for my life. I never could see myself being a missionary or professor. And I refused to let myself be seen as a pastor. But God has fueled the fire of his call on my life. He continues to guide my heart for ministry by the situations and people whom he has surrounded me with. By his grace alone could I take steps to overcome my fear of ministry and run hard after God.

Michelle Bodle is a first-year graduate student at Drew Theological School working toward a master of divinity degree. She is a member of the Central Pennsylvania Conference of The United Methodist Church.

Choosing a Simpler Path Wasn't an Option

Mary Ann Kaiser

I spent my early childhood years attending church every Sunday. I hated going. I remember trying to hide one of my dress shoes in hopes that if I couldn't find the proper attire, my mom might somehow decide we wouldn't go. It never worked; she always found the shoe.

It wasn't until I attended a Chrysalis retreat, a three-day spiritual renewal program, when I was fifteen that I finally realized what church was all about. It was then that I found God to be not a boring, strict, rule creator, but a loving and compassionate God with whom I could have a relationship.

When I returned home from this retreat with a burning desire to grow my relationship with God, I found myself wanting something different from the United Methodist church I had grown up in. I began attending a nondenominational church and enjoyed their obvious passion and style of worship. I was spiritually hungry and over the next few years I took in everything I could about God and who God is. In my junior year of high school, as I was thinking about college and what I wanted to do with my life, it just sort of dawned on me that I could simply not imagine a better vocation than that of ministry. Once the thought first entered my head, I was hooked.

Excited about my discovery, I eagerly shared my feelings with my youth pastor at the church I was attending. He politely informed me about the Scriptures that explained my role as a female in the

> When I began college I had given up on this calling regardless of the space it still took up in my mind and heart.

church, quickly crushing within me what I had been so sure of. I left that day very confused and distressed. But what could I do? The Scriptures seemed so clear. I continued to ask others in the church about these Scriptures and they all repeated the same thing, "Women are only to teach women."

When I began college I had given up on this calling regardless of the space it still took up in my mind and heart. I entered school as a marine biology major and hoped that God would at least bless me with a husband who was a pastor, so I could somehow still live out this desire in my heart.

College was filled with many challenges, including Introduction to Zoology. Though I had always been good at science, after only a few weeks of this class I was sure it wasn't the direction I should be going. I dropped the class and found myself again questioning what in the world I was supposed to be doing with myself. I still thought

Mary Ann Kaiser receives the blessing of a local king in Nibo, Nigeria, where she held a health conference at a church.

constantly about ministry, but continued to remind myself it was not a possible route for me.

My college roommate's father was now the senior pastor at the United Methodist church I had grown up in. Over time, the drive to the nondenominational church I had been attending became too much, and I was drawn back to my home church with my friend. I had never really gotten into the roots of the United Methodist tradition when I was younger, but now that I had returned I was eager to learn. I attended Bible studies, helped with the youth, participated in retreats, and found myself enjoying and believing in The United Methodist Church in a way I had not previously experienced.

Over Christmas break I joined a small group of people who were going caroling to the shut-ins from my church. We stood together and sang carols before a small, blind woman who could hardly hear, but still shed tears of joy and gratitude. All we had to offer her was the simple love of Christ in humble attempts at singing, but that love was enough for her. This woman, so in need of care and love, grabbed hold of my heart. I thought to myself that this is what the church is about, this is ministry, and this is what I want to be a part of. I could no longer fight the urge within me to make this my vocation. It didn't make sense that God would give me such a heart for ministry, and then tell me I couldn't pursue it. I wanted answers.

With much encouragement from my church pastors, I began the candidacy process, but still struggled with whether or not I was in the wrong. I was active in rebuilding the Wesley Foundation on my university campus and was given opportunities to preach often. I was already living out what I desired to do, but still I was challenged constantly by friends of other denominations or by random conversations with strangers who inquired about my future. I couldn't explain why I believed what I was doing was scripturally accurate and that bothered me. I researched, I read, I talked to clergywomen, and continued to battle with my understanding. Meanwhile, I was learning a great deal at school now that I had changed my major to organizational communication. It wasn't until later that I realized how this unknown major was so perfect for my future.

Though my classes were not religious, I was still learning a great deal about God, people, and myself. My classes broadened my mind and, more than anything, they began teaching me how to learn in a new way. I learned how to look beyond the surface level of things and into the depths. This was an invaluable skill for me when it came to interpreting Scripture and pursuing my heart. The more I was able to look at the Scriptures in context, the more I believed in what God had put on my heart the past years. God continued to become bigger and bigger to me, and as I learned more about his desire for his people—including justice, freedom, and human rights—the more I was drawn to missions.

A certified candidate for ordained ministry, I now find myself in Owerri, Nigeria, where I serve in HIV/AIDS prevention, preaching, and other ministries. I sit with peace and joy as I think about this calling that God surely has placed in my life, for God's work. Upon my return from my year in Nigeria, I will continue the pursuit of ordained ministry in seminary.

God's call is rarely an easy one to answer. At times it seems like there is every reason to deny it, to turn away from it, or to just choose a simpler path. However, to walk in the way that God has ordained for your individual life is always worth the struggle. God guides, God provides, and best of all, God is always with you.

Mary Ann Kaiser is a recent graduate of the University of West Florida where she majored in organizational communication. She is currently a missionary in Nigeria working in HIV/AIDS education and plans to continue her pursuit of ordination as a student at Garrett-Evangelical Theological Seminary.

Resources

Web

The General Board of Higher Education and Ministry • www.GBHEM.org
On this Web site, you will find information and resources related to
exploring God's call, seminary education, the Ministerial Education
Fund, candidacy, probation, scholarships, loans, extension ministries,
chaplaincy, and much more. Explore the community pages for
ways to connect with others engaged in the same work, or visit the
publications page to find printed resources that can assist you.

Explore Your Calling • ExploreCalling.org
This Web site builds bridges between those exploring ministry as
vocation and those who work as leaders or mentors in discernment
and leadership development. The Web site invites people to consider
God's call in their lives, provides answers to questions about candidacy
and ministry in The United Methodist Church, and enables ongoing
conversations that will "bridge" ministry candidates from one phase of
vocational exploration to the next. Visitors to the site may sign up to
receive updated information and highlighted features.

Young Clergy • www.umcyoungclergy.com

This interactive Web site for United Methodist clergy under the age of thirty-five provides an opportunity to discuss issues facing young clergy. The site includes videos that focus on young adults in ordained ministry and how young adults see the future of The United Methodist Church. There are links to blogs and other interactive discussions as well.

Is God Calling You? • IsGodCallingYou.org

This Web site can be used to explore and answer questions about a call to ministry in The United Methodist Church and the different expressions of ordained ministry through which to live out the call.

United Methodist Student Movement • www.umsm.org

The Web site for the United Methodist Student Movement, www.umsm.org, is one of diversity and inclusivity, connecting university and college students. On this Web site, you will find information about Student Forum, the annual leadership development event for college students, as well as links to Facebook groups and other information for United Methodist college students.

Young Adult Seminarians • www.yasn.org

The Young Adult Seminarians' Web site is the site for a network of United Methodist seminarians age thirty-five and under and those concerned with:

- supporting one another in their faith journeys;
- advocating for social justice;
- helping people discern their vocations;
- supporting persons involved in the candidacy process;
- providing a safe community in which issues relating to ministry as young adults can be addressed.

The Fund for Theological Education • www.thefund.org

The Fund for Theological Education's Web site, www.thefund.org, offers support to help gifted young people explore and respond to God's call in their lives. The mission of The Fund is to advance excellence as it encourages caring, capable, and courageous young adults from diverse backgrounds on their journey to become pastors and scholars—the next generation of leaders for the church.

The Lewis Center for Church Leadership • www.churchleadership.com

The center seeks to advance the understanding of Christian leadership and promote the effective and faithful practice of Christian leadership in the church and the world.

The Lewis Center serves as a resource for clergy and lay leaders, congregations, and denominational leaders. Through teaching, research, publications, and resources, the Lewis Center supports visionary spiritual leaders and addresses those key leadership issues so crucial to the church's faithful witness.

Books

Rubey, Sharon, ed. *The Christian as Minister: An Exploration into the Meaning of God's Call.* Nashville: The General Board of Higher Education and Ministry, The United Methodist Church, 2009.
> An introduction into the meaning of God's call to ministry, the vision for that ministry, and the opportunities The United Methodist Church offers to live out that call.

Roth, Robert. *Answering God's Call for Your Life: A Look at Christian Calls and Church Vocations.* Nashville: The General Board of Higher Education and Ministry, The United Methodist Church, 2006.
> A guide to help young people listen, discern, and understand God's call in their lives and its meaning for their life's work.

Clapper, Gregory S. *Living Your Heart's Desire: God's Call and Your Vocation*. Nashville: Upper Room Books, 2005.

> This author invites you to catch a glimpse of the mystery of who you are and what you are called to be and do as a child of God. Drawing from both Christian tradition and contemporary films, this book helps discern God's call by listening for the voice of God in your life.

Palmer, Parker J. *Let Your Life Speak: Listening for the Voice of Vocation*. San Francisco: Jossey-Bass, 2000.

> Through telling stories from his own life and the lives of others who have made a difference, Parker J. Palmer invites you to listen to the inner teacher and follow its leadings toward a sense of meaning and purpose.

Svennungsen, Ann M., and Melissa Wiginton, eds. *Awakened to a Calling: Reflections on the Vocation of Ministry*. Nashville: Abingdon Press, 2005.

> This is a book of honest and inspiring sermons on ministry vocation for those who want to explore the call to minister in our communities.